READING THE IMPOSSIBLE

Reading the Impossible

SEXUAL DIFFERENCE, CRITIQUE,
AND THE STAMP OF HISTORY

Elizabeth Weed

FORDHAM UNIVERSITY PRESS   NEW YORK 2024

Copyright © 2024 Fordham University Press

All rights reserved. No part of this publication may be reproduced, stored in a retrieval system, or transmitted in any form or by any means — electronic, mechanical, photocopy, recording, or any other — except for brief quotations in printed reviews, without the prior permission of the publisher.

Fordham University Press has no responsibility for the persistence or accuracy of URLs for external or third-party Internet websites referred to in this publication and does not guarantee that any content on such websites is, or will remain, accurate or appropriate.

Fordham University Press also publishes its books in a variety of electronic formats. Some content that appears in print may not be available in electronic books.

Visit us online at www.fordhampress.com.

Library of Congress Cataloging-in-Publication Data available online at https://catalog.loc.gov.

Printed in the United States of America

26 25 24   5 4 3 2 1

First edition

Contents

Prologue: Why read the impossible now?   1

1. States of Impasse   30
2. Reading Sexual Difference   42
3. Reading the Stamp of History   89
4. Reading the Feminist Impossible   120

   Coda   125

   ACKNOWLEDGMENTS   131

   NOTES   133

   BIBLIOGRAPHY   163

   INDEX   175

READING THE IMPOSSIBLE

Prologue
Why read the impossible now?

Taking to the Streets

In February 1969, Michel Foucault delivered his "What Is an Author" lecture to the French Philosophical Society. In the discussion that followed, Marxist sociologist Lucien Goldmann objected, unsurprisingly, that history is made by men, not discursive structures. Taking up some recent student graffiti proclaiming that "structures don't go out into the streets," Goldmann made his own proclamation: "You saw your structures in '68. . . . Those were people in the streets!" Jacques Lacan's quick and heated retort: "If the events of May demonstrated anything at all, they showed it was precisely that structures had taken to the streets!"[1]

According to Elisabeth Roudinesco, in taking sides with Foucault at the event, Lacan was setting the story straight on the famous graffiti. For in 1967–1968, she writes, liberal arts and linguistic students had vigorous debates about structuralism, and many (including Roudinesco herself) had "gone out into the streets 'in the name of' or 'because of' structures: they demanded to be taught about the work of Jakobson, Barthes, and the Russian formalists instead of old academic nonsense." By reading Lacan's retort in this context, Roudinesco sees it as a rather straightforward rebuke.[2]

Of course, there is another way of reading the Goldmann-Lacan dispute that sees the two addressing the same register of meaning. In that view, Lacan's retort is directly addressed to Goldmann's humanist opposition to structuralism. For Lacan, the key to what is happening in the streets lies in reading the work of the structures involved.

Indeed, in his "Impromptu" with Vincennes students in December 1969, Lacan is clear what his reading is. In the course of his exchange with exasperated students who demand to know what value Lacan's unruly discourse can have for the radical political change they seek, Lacan says:

> If you had a bit of patience, and if you really wanted our impromptus to continue, I would tell you that, always, the revolutionary aspiration has only a single possible outcome — of ending up as the master's discourse. This is what experience has proved. What you aspire to as revolutionaries is a master. You will get one.[3]

In warning the students to be wary of the master's discourse, Lacan is warning them not to be taken in by the fantasy of mastery, the fantasy the master signifier so inexorably produces, promising totalization and masking what is left over when totalization fails.

Decades later, and in very different circumstances, it is tempting to see structures in the streets once again. Today a branch of academic feminism that once brought poststructuralist and psychoanalytic formulations to bear on questions of sexual difference and sexuality is greatly diminished in size and influence, while at the same time, those formulations — the theoretical preoccupations of earlier days — have turned into memes that have taken to the streets. Arguments about access to bathrooms bring flashbacks of Lacan's two bathroom doors in "The Instance of the Letter in the Unconscious."[4] And if the pronoun "they," preferred by some to "he" or "she," does not correspond to theory's "split subject," it does bring down to earth the deconstructed binary. Where structuralism, post-structuralism, and deconstruction once labored to expose the masterful workings of the binary opposition, children can now enthusiastically embrace the non-binary. Of course, the current non-binary has to do primarily with "gender identity," which in turn leaves no doubt about the continuing presence of "gender," once a term of critique coined and debated by feminist theorists. And in the streets, as formerly in the academy, "gender" is construed in its relationship to the biological. If the anti-essentialism versus essentialism arguments that preoccupied the academy some fifty years ago were heated, they cannot compete in vigor and vitriol with debates between transgender activists and the feminists labeled TERFs.[5] Lest that particular terrain of battle seem parochial, consider the stakes that "gender" has accrued in the geopolitical sphere. Not only did Viktor Orbán banish well-established gender studies programs as part of his project to weaken Hungarian democracy, but alsoVladimir Putin regularly evokes "gender non-conformity" as fundamental to the corrosive Western influences that the war on Ukraine aims to abolish. And in domestic politics, of course, gender is the site of much anxiety, with "non-conformity" taken as the need or pretext for the banning of books and the suppression of once accepted educational curricula.

If, as Lacan asserts in 1969, the discursive structures are there to be read, how to read what we see in the streets today? That, indeed, is the question academic critics have been debating for at least two decades. Eve Sedgwick was one of the earliest to challenge the value of the then-dominant critical readings in her essay "Paranoid Reading and Reparative Reading."[6] Not only had the readings become formulaic and predictable applications of critical theory in her view, but what they revealed about social formations was actually visible, there to be seen: "How television-starved would someone have to be to find it shocking that ideologies contradict themselves, that simulacra don't have originals, or that gender representations are artificial?"[7]

Sedgwick grants that some critical demystifications may still have effects. But many, she writes, no matter how true or how convincing, have no effect at all, "and as long as that is so, we must admit that the efficacy and directionality of such acts reside somewhere else than in their relation to knowledge per se."[8] It was this contrast between critical knowledge, which seemed to have less and less to offer, and ubiquitous experiential knowledge that led many academics to abandon critique in favor of post-critical promises.

Early on, Bruno Latour supplied additional, unsettling evidence as to the exhaustion of critique. He pointed out that the demystification that had been the weapon of intellectuals "in the vanguard" was now a tool available to many. Just as the purveyors of critique could once expose "prematurely naturalized objective facts," so now could conspiracy theorists of all persuasions deploy that weapon. "Remember the good old days when university professors could look down on unsophisticated folks because those hillbillies naively believed in church, motherhood, and apple pie?" Well, things have changed, Latour writes, and in his village he is the one considered naïve for not knowing that 9/11 was the work of Massad and the CIA.[9] Theory has thus taken to the streets and, like a pathogen escaping from a lab, ushered in the era of "post-truth."

Impossibility

The turn away from critique by some in the academy has had its effects. With the changes in critical interest, feminist critical aims and fields of legibility have tended to contract. Where feminist work informed by post-structuralism and psychoanalysis once addressed phallic closure — the masculinist stranglehold on meaning — wherever it found it, much gender-identified criticism in the era of post-critique is thematically disciplined, looking to objects of inquiry deemed appropriate, such as those having to do primarily with women, gender, and sexuality. In other words, what was once a far-ranging critique of identity is now its disciplined affirmation.

This shift from critique to affirmation is by no means specific to feminism. But what does distinguish feminism is its particular relationship to Western ontotheology and structures of meaning. One of the earliest feminist insights was that in the history of Western thought and discourse "Woman" is inextricable from "Man," whereas the reverse is not the case.[10] While much of feminist history is absorbed with the epistemological and political effects of the knots in which Woman is caught, it was the explosion of post-structuralist and psychoanalytic critique in the France of the 1960s that rendered the impossibility of sexual difference a compelling theoretical conundrum.[11]

Among the factors fueling the French theoretical explosion was the excitement generated by structuralism, particularly structural linguistics and theorizations of language. As Michel Foucault writes in *The Order of Things*, before modernity, that is before the late eighteenth century, thought *is* representation, and language speaks the world. But from the late eighteenth century, from Kant onwards, representation becomes one form of thought among others. It is then that

Man finds himself in the paradoxical position of being both the subject of thought and its object, caught in an epistemological cleavage that can't be cured by logical coherence. If the break of modernity is a cleaving of epistemology and ontology, of language — in the broadest sense of *meaning* — and *being*, then what is lost is the Truth of metaphysics. Absent the truth of the logos, modernity confronts multiple modes of knowing. And what structuralism offered to the French theorists of the 1950s and 1960s was a rigorous way of better understanding knowledge-effects by looking at how structures of signification produce both meanings and their collapse.

On the one hand, then, a modern rupture of *meaning* and *being* that is impossible to close; on the other, exciting new ways to read meaning in the wake of rupture. And at the heart of this, the conundrum of sexual difference, a conundrum that seems to straddle both the ontological and epistemological sides of the impasse as a kind of limit-case of the impossibility of the modern episteme. Theoretically and politically the modern rupture of being and meaning offered feminists the opportunity to mobilize impossibility in new ways in order to challenge the seemingly impregnable truth of woman's subservience to man. For in discovering how the operations of phallic closure underpin Western cultural foundations, they also saw ways of resisting those foundations.

Of course, the explosion of structuralist theory had its effects in psychoanalysis as well. By bringing the work of structural linguistics to bear on Freudian psychoanalysis, Lacan addressed the break of meaning and being in a powerfully different register, raising the stakes for feminism. For how ever to combat the effects of misogynistic meaning without confronting the unconscious? The fact that grappling with the effects of the unconscious is not the same as reading the grammatological wiles of tropes and rhetoric did not deter many feminists, with the result that the branch of feminist inquiry informed by post-structuralism and psychoanalysis was for a time a force in the academy.

That time is long past, which is not to say that misogyny is neglected in the academy. There is certainly important academic work that looks at the intersectional operations of misogyny, just as there is important work in the streets: #BlackLivesMatter and #SayHerName; protests against *Dobbs v. Jackson*; resistance to the morality police in Iran; to the Taliban in Afghanistan. The question here is what value there might be in looking once again at the theoretical specificity of misogyny that emerges from the impossibility of sexual difference. Would such consideration contribute to intersectional readings? Would it encourage more critical reading of the gender and transgender wars?

Reading

One could argue that the specificity of misogyny has indeed been addressed, that its intractable power and persuasion has to do with the way sexual difference disrupts the comfortable closure of meaning, promoting violence that aims both to deny the disruption and to mask it. If the work of theorists has enabled us to understand a bit more fully the misogyny we see in the streets, what further demystification is needed? What is needed now beyond the confirmed examination of abuses? Certainly much of today's criticism bears witness to misogyny and to the related master discourses of gender, race, and colonialism.

For Stephen Best and Sharon Marcus, authors of "Surface Reading," "the way we read now," is indeed a textual bearing witness, an engagement with what is evident and perceptible as contrasted to the reading practices of the

1970s and 1980s that sought to expose hidden meanings.[12] Like Sedgwick, Best and Marcus argue that with changing times the demystifying work of critique has been rendered redundant. They argue, moreover, that with surface reading we necessarily relinquish the "freedom dream" that accompanied demystification for a more modest political realism.

If Sedgwick acknowledges the limits of once dominant modes of demystification, she does not share Best and Marcus's withdrawal from critique in the name of political realism. In fact, her continuing impatience with a reading that knows in advance what it will find leads her to look for more critique, not less. The difference for her is that the category of critique, and the change it can bring, is not limited to familiar modes of demystification. Hence, her interest in Silvan Tompkins and his notion of strong affective theories like paranoia that block weaker formations of meaning, preventing the unknown from appearing because saturated with the already known.

Sedgwick's faith in reading as a disruption of the known is informed by the ways earlier theorists engaged with how easily the epistemological gap is covered over by the known. Taking on the challenge of the modern episteme with no foundation for truth entailed transforming the practices of reading and writing. With the breakdown of language's representational powers, reading could no longer be relegated to the hermeneutic practice of seeking and elucidating meaning waiting to be found. It was thus that both reading and writing were transformed from instruments of interpretation to participants in the *production* of meaning. As Barbara Johnson notes, Roland Barthes undertook as early as 1953 in *Zero Degree Writing*, to distinguish between "text" and "work," with the former representing the subversion of meaning versus its closure, practice versus product, "significance-seeking process" versus "meaning-centered object."[13]

Reading as critique aimed, then, not to expose hidden meanings but to look at the conditions of possibility for their production in the form of structural effects. For Jacques Derrida, that entailed reading the play of *différance* in the text, namely the gap of difference and deferral at work in all meaning. For Lacan, it meant reading *après coup*, as the effects of signifying chains. These theorists, along with many others, afforded the hope that disrupting the force and logic of the Western symbolic order might somehow effect change in social and political spheres.

It is not surprising that so many decades later liberating the signifier seems for some to be a distant folly and that reading the impossible has been displaced onto the impossibility of critical reading itself. The critical passivity of "Surface Reading" is, after all, only a reflection of larger cultural and political concerns, post-critique having come of age with the full flowering of neoliberalism in the US. With the saturation of neoliberalism, the workings of advanced capitalism and concomitant social formulations have become more and more visible, for all to see. Along with deregulation, privatization, globalization, and other policies supporting the "freedom" of the markets, came an ideological valuation of the social atomization and pragmatic rationality that underlies "the way we read now."[14]

And yet, although post-critique gained much approbation in the academy, it was certainly not the only way "we" read now. For while post-critical acquiescence to neoliberal realism was gaining acclaim in some quarters, in others critique was deemed imperative. The 2014 special issue of *The Black Scholar* on "States of Black Studies" makes clear the importance of critique for the field. In his introduction to the issue, titled "Black Studies and Black Life," Alexander Weheliye draws a connection between the continuous murderous violence experienced by blacks and the work of black thought, "a strong recursive loop between these two domains that should not be submerged": "Black life is that which must be constitutively abjected — and as such has represented the negative ontological ground for the Western order of things at least for the last five hundred years...." It is crucial, he writes, to claim "the particular decolonizing critique developed within black studies. As Hortense Spillers and C.L.R. James have shown along with a host of other theorists of black studies, to construe black life as a parochial, ethnographic phenomenon rather than as 'the history of Western civilization' . . . simply reaffirms the very colonial structures black studies sets out to trounce."[15]

It was under the name of "Afro-pessimism" that black critique gained theoretical attention, thanks to its radical arguments as well as its coincidence with powerful political critiques of state violence such as #BlackLivesMatter.[16] In Frank Wilderson's recounting, Afro-pessimism grew out of efforts to understand the failure of the Left to deal with black suffering. True to his Marxist formations, Wilderson asked "where is the antagonism," referring to the class antagonism involved in the structural relations of the capitalist mode of production. Discussions with colleagues, including in particular Jared Sexton, led them to Orlando Patterson's *Slavery and Social Death*, Saidiya Hartman's *Scenes of Subjection*, David Marriott's work on Frantz Fanon and Lacan, and Hortense Spillers' "ungendering" of the black subjects. It was Sexton, he says, who finally suggested that the structural antagonism is not between blacks and whites but between "Blacks and the World," or, in Wilderson's terms, between Blacks and Humanity.[17]

For Afro-pessimism, the foreclosure of the Black from

Humanity is the effect of the structural violence of the transatlantic slave trade, putting the slave outside human value.[18] That is, Afro-pessimism's aim is not to reiterate the ways slavery strips the slave of human attributes — bodily autonomy, property, reproductive and social bonds. Nor does it aim to put the slave's injuries in competition with the sufferings of others. Its purpose is to expose the structural relations that produce the particular conditions of anti-black violence and racism that prevail long after Emancipation and six decades after Civil Rights. As Wilderson argues, the difference between the slave, on the one hand, and the Palestinian, or the Native American, or the subject of settler colonialism, on the other, is that the latter suffer dispossession of territorial sovereignty, while the former loses being. The difference between the black and the Jew is similarly the non-ontological status of the black: "Jews went into Auschwitz and came out as Jews. Africans went into the ships and came out as Blacks. The former is a Human holocaust; the latter is a Human *and* a metaphysical holocaust."[19] Anyone can be subjected to the experience of slavery, he writes. The distinction is between experience and "the ontology of slavery, which in modernity . . . becomes the singular purview of the Black."[20]

The term "ontological" can be confusing, of course, in that "ontology" is the primary object of critique in the reading of the split between epistemological meaning and ontological being. Jared Sexton addresses the confusion in his "Afro-Pessimism: The Unclear Word," by citing Robert Nichols:

> Ontology here does not refer to an essentialized structure of reality, that is, a rough synonym for metaphysics more generally. Instead, ontology refers to a particular form of analysis, one that affirms the idea that knowledge claims about the world are also

interpretations of what sorts of entities there are to be known, and, simultaneously, a certain ethical positioning of the subject of knowledge in relation to the world so interpreted. . . .[21]

Wilderson sees Afro-pessimism as a *political ontology*, doing for the black subject what Marx, in his political economy, does for the worker. The black in this reading, like the proletarian, is not a cultural identity but a structural positionality, the division being, for Wilderson, not Black/White but Black/non-Black.[22] The conceptual move, Sexton writes, is "from the empirical to the structural, or, more precisely, from the experiential to the ontological. . . ."[23] When asked what he would consider Afro-pessimism's major contribution, Wilderson says it is *"how we cannot think"* [citations continue from YouTube interview]. With American society and the academy so thoroughly wedded to the empirical, to evidence, to all that can be seen and documented, there is no way to know what we cannot know. What cannot be seen, he says, referring to Patterson's work, is what happens to all the violence — "oceans of violence" — required to establish and maintain the paradigms of subjection needed for any hierarchical social formation, violence that, once the hierarchy is in place, "goes under the table, turning into hegemony." To resist an oppressive system, there is more involved, Wilderson says, than the institutions, more than demonstrable words and actions. There are all the "tenacious fixations," all the unconscious and disavowed fantasies.

Sexton cautions that Afro-pessimism is not an abandonment of agency but an effort "to think rigorously about its conditions of possibility": "Afro-pessimism is not an intervention so much as it is a reading, or meta-commentary, on what we seem to do with, or how we relate to, what black creative intellectuals continue to generate without being able to bring fully into account."²⁴ In Sexton's view, then, rather than a new intervention, Afro-pessimism is a strong theoretical reading of what blocks the insights of black critique, past and present, from being brought "fully into account." One could say it aims to show the conditions of the *impossibility* of black critique's being able to effect change. And although the debates for and against Afro-pessimism have been heated, few disagree on the crucial need for critique.²⁵

Sexual Difference

If in the era of post-critique gender studies have become disciplined and predictably redundant, for Wilderson's Afro-pessimism, gender studies in any theoretical form are irrelevant if not reprehensible. In his reading, "gender" is a category that can only apply to non-black persons, an argument he makes with reference to Hortense Spillers's canonical "Mama's Baby, Papa's Maybe: An American Grammar Book." As with any strong reading, "ungendering" takes on different resonance in *Red, White, and Black* than it does in Spillers's essay. It is in response to the 1965 "Moynihan Report" that in 1987 Spillers offers a reading that historicizes the putative "pathology" of the black family. The reading takes her to slavery, where both female and male bodies "become a territory of cultural and political maneuver, not at all gender-related, gender specific." Where in non-captive life, she writes, there is a "profound intimacy of interlocking detail," at which point of convergence "biological, sexual, social, cultural, linguistic, ritualistic, and psychological fortunes join," in captivity this is all disrupted. Moreover, she adds, there is a central distinction between "captive and liberated subject-positions," having to do with the distinction between "flesh" and "body": "before the 'body' there is the 'flesh' that zero-degree of social conceptualization that does not escape concealment under the brush of discourse," and although it was African *bodies* that were stolen, "we regard this human and social irreparability as high crimes against the *flesh*, as the person of African females and African males registered the wounding."[26]

Wilderson's deployment of Spillers's reading is most forceful in his discussion of Kalpana Seshadri-Crooks's *Desiring Whiteness: A Lacanian Analysis of Race*, or more precisely, of Seshadri-Crooks's references to the work of Judith Butler. Of the numerous words of Butler that Wilderson cites from Shahadri-Crooks's book, the following, with Wilderson's emphases, will suffice: "Gender is the repeated *stylization of the body*, a set of repeated acts within a highly rigid *regulatory frame that congeals over time* to produce *the appearance of substance, of a natural sort of being*. A political genealogy of *gender ontologies*, if it is successful will deconstruct the substantive appearance of gender into its constitutive acts," allowing, Butler argues, for those acts to be grasped within "the compulsory frames set by the various forces that police the social appearance of gender."[27] Having found the perfect target, Wilderson heatedly attacks the presumption that such an analysis should ever apply to blacks, who are ungendered and deprived of bodies: "Here, an unforgivable obscenity is performed twice over: first, through the typical White feminist gesture that assumes all women (and men) have bodies, ergo all bodies contest gender's drama of value; and second, by way of the more recent, but no less common, assertions that the analysis of 'relations' between White and Black has a handy analog in the analysis of gendered relations."[28]

If Spillers's reading affords Wilderson the terms to position Butler's work as outside black ontology, it is Lacanian "lack" that informs his critique of "many White film theorists and White feminists," as in the list he offers: "Mary Ann Doane, Constance Penley, Kaja Silverman, Jacqueline Rose, Janet

Begstrom, and Luce Irigaray."[29] Like Marx, Lacan represents for Wilderson a necessary counterweight against positivist ideology. It is clear, he writes, that Lacan's break with the analytic establishment in his Rome Discourse "was a brake on what, in the 1950s was becoming psychoanalysis's slippery slope toward idealism and essentialism." Approving Lacan's critique of ego psychology and object relations theory, he praises what he characterizes as Lacan's brilliant intervention into the subject's alienation in language. Given that the subject in Lacan's theorization is not the ego, formed by imaginary identifications, but the subject born from unconscious effects of language, alienation "is literally what makes subjectivity possible." And, Wilderson continues, thanks to Lacan's psychoanalytic deployment of the distinction between empty speech (imaginary) and full speech (symbolic), "language can also be that agency through which the subject learns to live in a deconstructive relation to this alienation — learns to live with lack."[30]

The problem for Wilderson is that while the non-black analysand can have access to this form of "psychic liberation," access to the black is foreclosed. He is not arguing, he writes, that the unconscious does not exist. Nor is he "claiming that sentient beings, whether Human or Black, are not indeed alienated in the imaginary and the symbolic." Wilderson argues rather that while "alienation is an essential grammar underpinning Human relationality, it is an important but ultimately inessential grammar when one attempts to think the structural interdiction against Black recognition and incorporation . . . it is not a grammar that underwrites much less explains the absence of relationality."[31]

In his *Lacan Noir: Lacan and Afro-pessimism*, David Marriott offers a reading that differs from Wilderson's. One problem, he suggests, is that in focusing on the early Lacan of feminist film theory, Wilderson neglects later formulations of Lacan that turn on the very question of the *absence* of relationality: "But what has happened to the Lacanian 'real'? Is it not also opposed to meaning *as* relationality; is it not the impossibility of relationality as such?"[32] It is in Lacan's later work, Marriott writes, that he realizes the fantasy of a restoration within language: "What people want is not the resolution of a formerly repressed speech . . . nor do they want to be freed from the fantasy of that resolution." Above all, "what they don't want is the agitation that forces the mind to encounter the real of an unbearable vacancy. That is to say, we prefer the web of the symbolic chain to the senseless ruin of the real." Moreover, Marriott continues, at stake is the very ethical concern that drives Wilderson's project. The problem, he argues, is "not misunderstanding our desire, but blaming others—those deemed irreparably different—for the distress caused by those desires." This is why he argues that "we suffer not because we are alienated, but because we are alienated from our desires, in which we imagine a violent and vigorous onslaught by the Other's jouissance that repeatedly offends us, but which we choose to believe entices and seduces us. . . ."[33]

The impossibility of meaning that Lacan theorizes in his later work is not the negative (legible dialectically) or the ineffable (legible in religion or aesthetics), but the impossible—*ab-sens*. And it is in this work that Lacan theorizes sex and the sexual relation as residing outside meaning, and Woman (*La femme*) as occupying the position of meaning's "not-all." In Marriott's effort to find a "genealogy of slavery" somewhat different from that of Wilderson, Marriott reads the *nègre* as the Lacanian "less than nothing." However—and importantly—the relationship of the *nègre* to *ab-sens* is *not*, Marriott argues, that of the woman in Lacan's theorization, nor can it be read entirely through Lacan. Marriott's effort to read the relationship of the *nègre* to "the primordial lack out of which meaning is woven" and into which the black is cast down,[34] is an effort to think blackness through Lacan, who, as Marriott writes, is *indifferent* to it. "The book is written, then, out of a certain distrustful love of Lacan," along with a reading of Frantz Fanon's similar love of — and break from — Lacan. "Limited in every respect, but aware of its limitations: perhaps there is an origin and image here of a certain black reading?"[35]

Although Marriott seeks to think through Lacan and Fanon the "racist fantasy of the real," his reading is, as he says, different from the Lacanian thinking that yields what we might call the "misogyny of the real."[36] Both turn on the impossibility of *ab-sens*, but with different effects. To collapse them as analogous is to lose the importance of their specificity. The challenges that Marriott's Afro-pessimist reading presents to feminist theory are, thus, vast. On the one hand, there is the challenge to *recall* the impossibility of sexual difference, lost long ago to a positivist notion of "gender." And second, there is the question of how to think the convergence of "racist fantasies of the real" and the "misogyny of the real." While "Reading the Impossible" is a modest attempt to address only the first, the stakes for doing so are inextricable from the second.

In his criticism of the "typical White feminist gesture" that assumes blacks have the same relationship to gender as non-blacks, Wilderson expresses an anger, which, though symptomatically excessive, has some resonance with the frustration and rage of black feminist theorists at the limits of white feminist theory. However, that frustration has never been only with white feminist theory, but with male theory as well that is seemingly blind to feminist concerns. And the problem some black feminist theorists have with Afro-pessimism is that the critique seems to stop with the turn of "ungendering." In her essay "Black Feminist Theory for the

Dead and Dying," Patrice Douglass powerfully evokes the anguished double-bind of black women confronted, on the one hand, with the obvious inadequacy of "gender," and, on the other, with a radical critique of blackness that ends with the "ungendering" of the captive body. Although separated by decades, Douglass's essay can thus be said to echo the 1982 black feminist anthology *All the Women Are White, All the Men Are Black, But Some of Us Are Brave*.[37]

Douglass frames her essay with the 2010 murder of Korryn Gaines by the Baltimore SWAT.[38] Gaines's death is like those of so many women, eclipsed in public discourse by the deaths of black men. The problem with gender politics, Douglass writes, is that gender theory envisions violence against women in universalizing terms, a vision exposed by the 2017 Women's March on Washington. Produced as a cross-racial coalition honoring scores of black women activists, she argues that the March only reinforced the narrative of "violence against women" as universal in structure and kind. That assumption of universality requires the kind of correction that Sylvia Wynter calls for, Douglass writes, citing Wynter's insight that "the codification of gender concerns within a feminist framework . . . circumvented and ignored the 'negro question,' such that gender functions as a genre of Man."[39]

In Douglass's view, what Afro-pessimism has to offer introspections into gender is a critical intervention into the logic and discourses of universality: that "while there is no place in history where all women have stood subjected equally to violence, there is such a place for the black, the hold of a slave ship." And in that context, "Black gender as a theorem, not a thing, dismantles the predicate of gender." The problem for the black feminist, however, is "how to account for the gravity of gender violences that lack a proper name."[40]

It is here that Douglass locates the fault line in Afro-pessimism: "There is a question announcing itself through the halls and silos of the academy, 'does Afro-pessimism adequately deal with the question of black gender?'. . . . Is it theoretically silent on this point, when in all other iterations it is theoretically quite loud?"[41] However crucial Afro-pessimism's thinking on the foreclosure of blackness, the "conceptual misstep," Douglass argues, is to stay at a structural level without a theorization of subjectivity that might account for gender. "While performance is important to the imperative concerns of race and gender," she writes, alluding to Wilderson's wholesale refusal of "white" feminist theorization of performativity, Afro-pessimism is wrong in not staking "an investment in mediating Blackness" through "variously and unconsciously interpellated identity or as a conscious social actor."[42] Lacking such critical tools, she sees women like Korryn Gaines dying, trapped in the impasse between blackness and gender as a category of the Human.[43]

The impasse Douglass points to is all the more striking when one considers the trajectory of the "gender" that was once employed as a term of critique. When taken up by feminist theorists some decades ago, "gender" was invoked as a way of freeing Woman from her onto-theological Human position: the place of the body eternally subservient to the spirit of Man. To borrow Douglass's words, "gender as a theorem, not a thing," was employed by feminists to displace Woman, and to expose all the conscious and unconscious effects the fantasy of Woman has in the cultural workings of "gender." In dismantling the predicate, they showed the catachresis left in its stead, that grammatical term for non-foundational meaning. For Joan Scott, Judith Butler, and the theorists who followed, catachrestic "gender" was a tool of disruption.[44]

The problem was that catachresis turned out to be more manageable than not. In the preface to the 1999 revised edition of *Gender and the Politics of History*, Scott describes the difficulty that "gender" presented to the 1995 UN Conference on Women. So great was the controversy that a subcommittee of the US House of Representatives held hearings in which Republicans and assorted delegates aired their concerns about the threat "gender" presented to morality and family values in its challenge to biology and everything "natural." Finally a compromise was reached with a "Statement on the Commonly Understood Meaning of the Term 'Gender'" appended to the UN conference's Program of Action. However, and strikingly, in the compromise statement there was no definition of its meaning, just a tautological reference to "its generally accepted usage." Scott comments that despite the furor, the term itself was by then beside the point:

> In ordinary usage, "gender" had become a synonym for the differences between the sexes, both ascribed and "natural." Although it still could provoke heated debate and widespread anxiety among feminists as well as their critics, "gender" no longer transformed or destabilized political discourse....[45]

So it was in the academy that queer theory gave up on "gender" as a disruptive category, looking to "sexuality" to disturb the peace.[46] So it is today that the "gender" that transgender activists seek to disrupt is gender "in its generally accepted usage."

And so it is that "gender" as the fully relational designation of the difference between men and women—whether ascribed or natural—persists as the "underpinning of Human relationality," incommensurable with blackness theorized as *ab-sens*, as outside the Human.

While "race" was widely recognized as a pseudo-scientific term of eugenics, the doubly catachrestic "black gender" was not treated with such clarity. To use Wynter's words, although black gender was not entirely ignored, it was circumvented in symptomatic ways. The 1997 *Female Subjects in Black and White: Race, Psychoanalysis, Feminism* is illustrative. The editors of the volume admirably chose to foreground the tensions that had been evident at the 1992 Santa Cruz conference where the essays originated. Rather than framing the contributions as producing reconciliation, they chose to "represent the disjunctures, as well as the intersections" of disparate critical agendas.[47]

The opening essay of the collection is Ann du Cille's "The Occult of True Black Womanhood." In the essay, du Cille famously analyzes the complicated and vexing effects of the intense commodification of black women's writing and scholarship in the 1990s. "Within and around the modern academy," she writes, racial and gender alterity has become a hot commodity that has claimed black women as its principle signifier." The essay is not, she insists, "yet another black womanist indictment of white feminists who can do no right and men who can do only wrong."[48] Indeed, in analyzing what is so disturbing — and infuriating — about the frenzied consumption of the Other centering on the black woman, du Cille points to a commodity that is oxymoronic but everywhere for sale: black woman as *essentialism commodified*.

The commodity du Cille identifies is oxymoronic because, as Marx explains in careful detail at the beginning of *Capital*, what transforms a normal object into a commodity is the *loss* of its essence. That is, the value of the commodity stems not from what it is, but from its worth in exchange.[49] And there, in the 1990s, du Cille writes, black women were called on to "sell back to the dominant culture its constitution of our always already essentialized identity."[50] Of course, the essence of black womanhood was a fantasy, but a hot commodity nonetheless. And perfectly characterized by du Cille as "occult," given Marx's comparison of the "mystical character" of the commodity, which seems to emanate its own value, to the mysterious fetish.

It is striking how du Cille's essay resonates decades later: the white women drawn to black writers such as Toni Morrison because "they concretize and make vivid a system of oppression"; and the white person eager to show how racist she is not. "This, then," du Cille writes, "is the final paradox and the ultimate failure of the evidence of experience to be valid — to be true — black womanhood must be legible as white or male; the texts of black women must be readable as maps, indexes to someone else's experience, subject to a seemingly endless process of translation and transference."[51]

The Stamp of History

Karl Marx invokes the "stamp of history" when discussing the historical conditions "necessary that a product may become a commodity," conditions that render the *commodity of labor* invisible to the bourgeois political economist. Marx shows how the thinking of the bourgeois economist stumbles at the impasse created by two incongruous formulations: the pre-capitalist question of the maintenance and reproduction of the human laborer himself, and the capitalist abstraction and exchange of labor for money (labor-power). Asking what the price of labor is in a capitalist market, the bourgeois economists go on to ask the cost of producing or reproducing the laborer, a question that moves from one problematic to another, or, as Marx writes: "The question unconsciously substituted itself in Political Economy for the original one; for the search after the cost of production of labour as such turned in a circle and never left the spot."[52]

Thus Marx shows how apparently straightforward categories of meaning change with changing historical conditions.[53] If those outside the dialectical tradition have characterized the stamp as a more or less direct causal relationship between the economic base and the cultural superstructure, the dialectical Marx offers a more interesting understanding. While the passage cited above shows the effects of economic formations on systems of meaning, the reverse is also always at play in Marx's thinking, as in the first chapter of *Capital*, for example, where he argues that without the bourgeois notion of "equality" among people, the principle of equivalence necessary for the commodity form would be "unthinkable."[54]

It is this inextricable connection among economic, epistemological, and social-political structures that Louis Althusser probes in *Reading Capital*.[55] And it is the epistemological dimension that Althusser's student, Michel Foucault, brings to life so vividly in *The Order of Things*. Focusing on the historical specificity of *knowing* and *representing*, he shows how dramatically systems of knowledge change from the classical period to modernity.[56] A little more than a decade later (*Les Mots et les choses* was published in 1966), Foucault delivered a series of lectures at the Collège de France, including lectures on American neoliberalism, which, unlike that of Margaret Thatcher's Britain, had not yet displayed its full effects. In Foucault's analysis, America afforded conditions for neoliberalism unique in their favorability:

> . . . American liberalism is not . . . just an economic and political choice formed and formulated by those who govern and within the government milieu. Liberalism in America is a whole way of being and thinking. It is a type of relation between the governors and the governed much more than a technique

of governors with regard to the governed. Let's say,
if you like, that whereas in a country like France disputes between individuals and the state turn on the
problem of service, of public service, [in the United
States] disputes between individuals and government
look like the problem of freedoms. I think this is why
American liberalism currently appears not just, or
not so much as a political alternative, but let's say as
a sort of many-sided, ambiguous global claim with a
foothold in both the right and the left.[57]

It is for these reasons that Foucault sees the US as particularly ripe for neoliberalism. He goes on to evoke Fredrick Hayek as saying: "We need a liberalism that is a living thought. . . . It is up to us to create liberal utopias, to think in a liberal mode, rather than present liberalism as a technical alternative for government"; after which Foucault adds his own words: "Liberalism must be a general style of thought, analysis, and imagination."[58]

Neoliberalism as a style of thought, analysis, and imagination has by now been generalized everywhere in the US including, of course, in education. After a relatively slow start, the transformation of the American university from one still rooted in the German model to today's market-driven corporation was dramatically rapid. When Bill Reddings's *The University in Ruins* appeared in 1996, the full corporatization of the institution was not yet complete.[59] It was the early years of 2000 that saw the accelerated transfer of institutional governance from the faculty to administrative management and corporate boards. There is no surprise, then, that given the university's concern with the market value of knowledge, the "theory" of the past is seen as having limited value today. Proponents of post-critique refer precisely to the irrelevance of once dominant critique. Times have changed, concerns are different, and there is nothing more for critique to expose.

The "stamp of history" offers an alternative way of viewing the relationship between past and present. If the insights of "theory" seem to have nothing new to offer, one could say it is because the earlier theoretical insights into the modern episteme served to expose *the conditions of possibility* for a flourishing neoliberalism. Just as commodity logic is now common sense, so does neoliberal discourse know all it needs to know about mobilizing a non-foundational, relational language of differences, proceeding with a remarkable mastery of formalism. What matters in neoliberal discourse is not the ground, the "truth," or even the verisimilitude of a statement, but its affective transactional value.

With such an adaptive discourse at work promoting neoliberalism's identity politics, it is difficult to mount a counter discourse. Equally difficult to counter is the extent to which identity has come to be the unquestioned ground of the political.[60] Even those who acknowledge — or defend — identities as ascribed, grant those identities a legitimacy as strong as any authorized by natural or divine law. At one time Marxist critics were concerned to decry the naturalization of the commodity. Today it is identity that allows the logic of capital to proceed untroubled. And if, as Adolph Reed argues, the naturalization of attributed identities fuels neoliberalism, Wendy Brown's 1995 *States of Injury* shows what fuels the naturalization.[61] That is, with biology and the divine having lost firm ground, Brown shows how political identities today are bolstered through the relational attribution of injury, which in turn bolsters the neoliberal naturalization of identity. The identities that are grounded in injury (injuries of gender, race, class, and so forth) are driven by Nietszchean *ressentiment*, or the conviction that the other is responsible for one's suffering. And it is the state, Brown shows, that produces and promotes the state of injury. Why look to *structural* injustices when the *relational* other is so close at hand, the other that is both essential for one's identity (I am not that other) and the source of injustice? And why relinquish victimization when its pleasures and rewards are everywhere to be found?

The politics of identification, framed through relational discourses of identity and difference, are indeed endlessly effective in their wiliness, supporting *ressentiment* both consciously and unconsciously. In coalition politics, for example, one must find others with injuries that resemble but don't trump one's own. In *Ethics of the Real*, Alenka Zupančič quotes Lacan on the topic: "My egoism is quite content with a certain altruism, altruism of the kind that is situated on the level of the useful. . . . What I want is the good of others provided that it remain in the image of my own."[62]

A related problem is the notion of empathy, that capacity to imagine and understand the suffering of others. In *Scenes of Subjection*, Hartman exposes its trickiness. No matter how well-intentioned the empathic evocations of the sufferings of the slave in abolitionist representations, the very condition that enables the identification — that renders the suffering fungible — is the slave's captivity. Moreover, no matter how extreme the scene of suffering, there is no escaping the sadistic pleasure that stealthily fuels the horror of the imaginary witness. And with identity politics come also the vicissitudes of the marketplace of injury. The logic of exchange value is easily mastered. Since it is not some solid ground that produces value and meaning, something tangible, the logic of equivalence is always available and particularly useful in rewriting history: men can display the injuries wrought by too much feminism, white children the trauma produced by hearing too much about slavery and racism.

Although it may make sense to posit the critical relationship between earlier theoretical discourses and that of neoliberalism, it is nonetheless striking to contrast the challenge that the modern episteme posed to the 1960s and beyond with the insouciance of today's neoliberal discourse. Slovenian sociologist Primož Krašovec offers some helpful genealogical perspectives in his essay, "Neoliberal Epistemology — From the Impossibility of Knowing to Human Capital." Krašovec's discussion ranges from the work of Frederick Hayek, whose very different views on the impossibility of human knowledge led him to embrace the rationality of the market; to Michael Polanyi, who argues that scientific research should function analogously to the free market; to Peter Drucker, whose management theories saw education as capital investment.[63] Of interest here is Hayek's view of "The Use of Knowledge in Society," to cite the title of his influential article that appeared in *The American Economic Review* in 1943. While Foucault and other continental theorists see the split of the modern episteme as historically driven, Hayek has no such historical analysis; for Hayek, the "dispersal and fragmentary nature" of knowledge "just is so."[64] As Krašovec writes, at some point in "The Use of Knowledge in Society," Hayek leaves economics behind, absorbed in epistemology: "what do people know, how do they know what they know, what is the ontological status of knowledge, how is knowledge socially acquired and distributed."[65] Convinced that the imperfect and flawed knowledge behind social planning and "utopian" socialist projects could never be equal to complex, unpredictable changes nor to the tempo of technological innovation, Hayek looks to the market to process information and fragmentary knowledges. In his view, the free market and price system are not "a result of conscious human endeavors but organic institutions, which have evolved spontaneously as unplanned byproducts of complex interactions of social actions of individuals."⁶⁶ It is thus, Krašovec argues, that Hayek's epistemological preoccupations, unlike his views of the market, dismissed long ago, have contributed to the neoliberal dismantling of society and democracy.

It is a bit disconcerting to find echoes of Hayek in Best and Marcus's "Surface Reading," where, in the light of the failure of critique to produce meaningful or actionable knowledge, they express a skepticism "about any kind of transcendent value we might use to justify intellectual work." Better to let go of the "critical styles" of the second half of the twentieth century that were "marked by a utopian strain and a striving for redemption" and to approach objects of study with a neutral concern for simple accuracy of description. Better to recognize the limits of reading and let the object speak for itself.⁶⁷

What is so curious about a post-critical argument such as that of "Surface Reading," is the readiness with which it posits reading as captive of its subject matter. Most proponents of critique are not theoretically naïve; most do not view reading as a pre-critically transparent practice. But once reading is deemed no longer capable of revealing anything hitherto unknown, it becomes, like Hayek's knowledge, the servant of the evident.

It is here that surface reading suffers from its own inability to see, from its failure to recognize that the evident is limited in more than one register. A neoliberal discourse with no depth does indeed serve very well the needs of a market that still, in the age of financialization, operates according to the logic of abstraction that Marx derives in his analysis of the commodity. But while the modern episteme with its impossible break serves the market, there is an impossibility left over, an excess impossibility not contained in neoliberal discourse. A surface reading might be able to show catachresis in action, but how to read "the racist fantasy of the real" or the misogyny of the real? How in Marriott's words to grasp what is produced by the "real of an unbearable vacancy," "the senseless ruin of the real"? At stake is not something that escapes meaning, not something that could somehow be represented in a signifying order that, as Zupančič shows, "is co-extensive with a gap."[68] There is no meaning to be had in being. All one can do is try to read the effects of the impossible.

Hoping to return once more to the misogyny of the real, "Reading the Impossible" looks again at the Derrida-Lacan debate on the question of sexual difference, with their very different readings of its impossibility. But it returns to that debate for another reason as well: to recall the *critical value* of reading.

1
States of Impasse

In a *Guardian* opinion essay following the 2016 US presidential election, Jacqueline Rose reflects on the ways Donald Trump might undermine decades of feminist success in challenging the "crassest version of masculinity." The revived crassness seems, indeed, so natural as to be inevitable. Rose writes of one female Trump supporter who, when asked how she could vote for a candidate with so little respect for women, answered with a shrug: "Well, I am a woman and he is a man," an observation apparently reassuring in its commonsense realism. As Rose comments, "If Trump's populism relied on nostalgia — making America great again, restoring jobs and communities felt to be lost — nostalgia for sexual certainty, however oppressive, violent or degrading, was one of the powerful cards he played." Quoting one illustrative tweet that read "If you want a country with 63 genders vote Clinton; if you want a country where men are men and women are women, vote Trump," she quips that a little misogyny might seem a small price for dispelling confusion about sexual identity, "for allowing us to hold on to the illusion that, deep in our sexual being where nothing in fact can be certain, we all know unequivocally who and what we are."[1]

While the victory of Donald Trump raises far-reaching questions having to do with the effects of the neoliberal order of global capitalism and the undermining of democratic institutions, the nostalgia for sexual certainty that Rose points to cannot be ignored. Indeed, in subsequent years, that nostalgia has opened the way to triumphalist, fully embraced misogyny, along with heated opposition to any expression of sexuality that challenges the supposed stability of gender and the inviolability of the heterosexual union. Feminist theorists can only wonder, yet again, at just how *available* such appeals are, how easily they are mobilized, how readily recognized, like old acquaintances absent perhaps but not forgotten. And once again we can remark how redundant all the feminist theorizing can seem when it meets head-on with such old acquaintances. How to respond? Politically, of course. And yet, Rose warns that a political response in itself is not sufficient. In her view, Trump succeeded in what the right has long done so well, namely license "the obscenity of the unconscious." For her, to counter unconscious enticements with even the deftest of political parries is to forget the intractable power of the question of sexuality.

Rose's warning carries echoes of Luce Irigaray's 1977 admonition that there can be no lasting feminist victories until "our age" comes to grips with sexual difference. Writing in 1984, Irigaray goes so far as to say: "Sexual difference is probably the issue in our time which could be our "salvation" if we thought it through."[2] While many feminist theorists undertook to think through the issue, it cannot be said that anything like salvation was achieved. Decades after Irigaray's admonition, the question of sexual difference reached an impasse among the feminist theorists who debated it, with a divide separating those who theorized the impossibility of sexual difference through the split of difference and those who looked to differences. In other words, the debates ended in a divide over a divide, a deadlock.

"Deadlock" is an apt term given that debates between the two sides are a thing of the past. While the two theoretical positions more or less survive in specialized corners of academic feminism, they have been largely displaced inside and outside the academy by the very different popular discourse of gender multiplicity, a view that encompasses a number of identity discourses, including queer, straight, genderqueer, and trans. At first glance it may seem that the old theoretical split between "differences" and "difference" has taken to the streets. This is not, however, the case, for while the earlier feminist theorists on both sides of the debate grappled with the impossibility of ever knowing the truth of sexuality, both sides in today's debates share discourses of certainty.

It is instructive to look more closely at the apparent impasse Rose refers to in the popular sector, between those who embrace multiple genders and those who are certain that men are men and women are women. In doing so, one finds that splits and strains having to do with questions of knowledge, sexuality, and identity are not as neatly divided as one might think. That is, it turns out that the world where men are men and women are women is not the only one that holds on to "the illusion that deep in our sexual being . . .we know unequivocally who and what we are." One can find similar vigorous assertions of certainty in the world of gender multiplicity as well. Take the heated debates between some feminists and some trans advocates. Although there are (cis) feminists who welcome transwomen into the fold, there are others who object to the trans appropriation of womanhood. And although there are trans theorists and activists who see "trans" as precisely not the discovery and recovery of certainty, there are others who view trans identity as liberation from entrapment in the wrong body. Hence, one can find debates in which, on the one hand, transwomen replace biology with an inherent truth that nature emphatically got wrong and, on the other, feminists who once worked to delink gender and biology now claiming the specificity of biological womanhood. It is in such cases that certainty seems to be at stake on both sides: a certainty that "trans" is the other of biology and that "cis" is inseparable from it.[3]

The certainty at stake in both camps is secured by two types of knowledge that while opposed, nevertheless function similarly. The tweeted knowledge about men and women that allows us "to know unequivocally who and what we are" derives from the "outside," as it were, from "nature." It is something that can go without saying. By contrast, the knowledge that authorizes the gender identities in question is unapologetically subjective. This knowledge does not go without saying; to the contrary, it grounds a politics of identity dependent on the unfettered insistence on "who and what we are," even if the identity we claim is fluid and ambiguous.

It is striking how these current gender identity claims depart from the assumptions that underpinned the feminist academic debates of some decades ago. For theorists on both sides of the difference/differences argument, as well as for theorists of gender, issues of identity and self-evidence were *problems*, questions to be pursued, not truths to be defended. Moreover, identity politics itself did not carry the discursive certainty it has now. Today's discourses of identity take different forms and serve different functions than they did even a decade ago, and changing configurations of identity entail changing registers of legibility.

In her 1994 essay on "Women and Allegory," in a subsection titled "Allegory and Identity Politics," Barbara Johnson characterizes the then current identity politics as "the politics of representativity," of speaking "as a,"[4] which she characterizes as allegorical rather than symbolic, referring to the distinction made by Paul de Man in another context: "Whereas the symbol postulates the possibility of an identity or identification, allegory designates primarily a distance in relation to its own origin, and, renouncing the nostalgia and the desire to coincide, it establishes its language in the void of this temporal distance."[5]

If one views identity politics as an allegorical formulation, its truth, Johnson writes, may be seen as "contractual" rather than "constitutive," and the bearer of the identity as the representative of a position, not the personification of a trait. The example Johnson uses to illustrate the section of the "Women and Allegory" essay is the strike by Derrick Bell, the first African American man tenured at Harvard Law School, against the Law School. In 1987, Bell wrote *And We Are Not Saved*, a series of reflections on the failures of the US Civil Rights movement seen through the chronicles of an allegorical black woman lawyer, Geneva Crenshaw.[6] Several years later, Bell left Harvard to protest its failure to hire and tenure an African American woman. That the example Johnson uses has to do with race as well as gender is significant. Even today the earlier dimension of identity politics that Johnson describes as contractual can be found in antiracist movements such as #BlackLivesMatter. Where it is diminished is in identity politics having to do primarily with gender or sexuality. There, what tends to drive the politics is not primarily what identity can achieve "as a," but what the deeply felt identity in question deserves in the form of recognition.

In the case of sexual identity, truth certainly has always had a special status, with the sense of lived experience trumping any putative theoretical distance. But the problem for feminists some decades ago was that the unquestioned lived experience of *some* was projected onto an unquestioned idea of nature's truth, a problem that called for a critical challenge to the transparency of both *nature* and *experience*. In the current time of identity politics, however, a challenge to the authority of lived experience can be construed as an intolerable affront. Whether the identity in question is that of gender, transgender, genderqueer, or sexual orientation, the subjective sense of truth can be the final word.[7] Of course, I refer here not to the actual nature of the lived experience but to the particular discourse of certainty that prevails in some circles, even if the truth involved is expressed in the service of subjective ambiguity.

A 2014 post by Eloise Brook on "The Conversation" illustrates how language is seen to ensure a transparent relationship between words and subjective truths. Titled "Trans, transgender, cisgender: we are what we name ourselves," the post takes on the question of language and gender diversity. Brook comments on the way "changing language reflects . . . changes in social attitudes." Language is crucial indeed for recognizing the new: "Language used in this way is as inexorable and beautiful to observe as a volcanic chain rising out of the ocean to make new islands." Brook looks at the different terms people use to describe themselves as "experiments in fashioning new words and meaning," and recognizes that the flux and shifts in language can cause intense debate. However, although language may be debatable — terms may be found inadequate or offensive — what it describes is never in question. It is language's job to reflect the truth of identity.[8]

Insofar as language in Brook's account attempts to render lived identity as faithfully and effectively as possible, it corresponds to the constitutive side of Johnson's distinction between constitutive and contractual terms—terms, Johnson writes, "caught up in the question of whether truth and falsehood are themselves constitutive or contractual, denominative or imperative." With the contractual, when a person speaks "as a," Johnson argues, the attempt is to align true/false with right/wrong, actively engaging the aporia of truth and politics.[9] With much of today's politics of gender identity, there is little engagement with the aporia; true/false takes the fore, and the once performative alignment of true/false and right/wrong gives way to an energetically defended constative, albeit one that is itself performative. That is to say, truth functions here as it does elsewhere in neoliberal discourse: as fully transactional.[10]

Transactional is indeed the key word, for the gender struggles that turn on an unassailable certainty have been produced by the zero-sum identitarian logics that fuel the populist right. The difference, of course, is that the right draws on the power of normativity. And in this neoliberal world where mastery and control are so crucial, norms that were challenged not long ago are once again potent instruments in the hands of the powerful. In conservative states in the US, there are increasingly successful efforts to banish expressions of transgender through legislation, the control of public education, and the banning of books, as well as renewed opposition to sexual orientation. And in authoritarian societies worldwide, gender has become a favored political tool, as in Hungary, where Victor Orbán eliminated a respected gender studies program from the Central European University, proclaiming that in the view of the Hungarian government people are born either men or women.

If uncompromising confrontation is currently the dominant form of oppositional politics, it is not clear what would constitute political change on the progressive side of the struggle, where, to use Barbara Johnson's words, the proliferation of identitarian truths "clogs" the social field. Writing in 1994, Johnson comments: "To the extent that identity politics presupposes that people are personifications of their readable traits, that each person represents synecdochally — and 'symbolically' in de Man's sense — the group to which he or she belongs, the social text would indeed become balkanized and clogged with its own readability."[11]

The social text clogged with its own readability is one in which multiple identities speak for themselves. Of course, the phenomenon that speaks for itself is just what Best and Marcus see as the preferred object of criticism in "Surface Reading." Following their argument, to see the collapse of the allegorical onto the symbolic as an unfortunate loss would be to impose old protocols on the way we read now. Why look to distancing operations in a text? Why ask reading to do political work in these times, when it is evident that the critical pretensions of intellectual work were overblown in the era of critique, promising insights that were not delivered. The more modest "surface reading" would attend to "what is evident, perceptible, apprehensible in texts; what is neither hidden nor hiding."[12] Indeed, the discourse of gender multiplicity virtually calls for a surface reading: a discourse that speaks for itself, that vigorously asserts the constative role of language, and that blankets the social field with its emphatic readability.

However, if one *does* attend to the readability of the surface of the discourse and not to any hidden dimension, it is hard not to notice the degree of energy that fuels the foundational assertions of today's gender identities, an energy that gives their conviction its particular coloring. One might say that what animates the truth of the gender identities is a twist particular to these times having to do once again with how one knows. That twist, that insistence on a derived truth, participates in a cultural logic of knowing that is *fetishistic*.

A knowledge can be called fetishistic when its object has a particular counterfeit relationship to conventional valuation that is simultaneously acknowledged and denied. And although two of the famous formulations of fetishism — commodity fetishism and sexual fetishism — belong to different theoretical paradigms, they share structural similarities that the current discourse of gender multiplicity can be said to draw on.

Commodity fetishism is the sleight of hand that mystifies value. Produced by labor-power, which is itself sold as a commodity, the value of the commodity is determined not by some inherent worth (like the wooly warmth of a coat), but by its relationship to other commodities. Hence, Marx's famous description of the mystification that occurs when a social relation among men assumes the "fantastic form of a relation between things," things that seem to magically produce their own value.[13] And again, where critics once worked to expose the treachery of the commodity, in these times the sleight of hand no longer matters. Inherent value or exchange value, it all amounts to the same thing: commodity fetishism has become "second nature" and fetishistic logic is a modern way of knowing familiar to all. As to the sexual fetish, it derives its power from the fetishist's simultaneous acknowledgment and disavowal of the female's missing penis. As an embodiment of this simultaneous acknowledgment and disavowal, the fetish thus solves a big problem, allowing the fetishist to maintain his initial belief while at the same time protecting himself from castration.

One might say that multiplicity discourses take something from both fetishisms. In substituting subjective truth for nature, the insistence on personal conviction has the same affective force as appeals to the truth of "nature," that realm of the "innate." And here the gender discourse has something of the flavor of sexual fetishism in that its assertive energy falls on the truth of the *substitution*. What is so remarkable about the logic of fetishism is this further twist: that neither with the commodity nor with sexual fetishism *is anything actually substituted*, nor is there any underside, any hidden presence to trouble the surface. The classic sexual fetish is substituted for a maternal phallus that was never there in the first place, much as in the most emphatic of identitarian discourses an achieved truth of gender or sex is substituted for a truth of nature that was never there. With the commodity, it may seem as if use value were there in the first place only to be banished by exchange value. But for Marx, that is precisely the trick that the logic of capital plays on what precedes it. In tracing the workings of the commodity, Marx shows how it is only retroactively with the emergence of the value of equivalence (value as equivalent to abstracted labor power) that such a notion as "use value" appears. To attach a notion of precapitalist "use" to the term "use value" is to bring together apples and oranges — as only fetishism knows how.

If those in the tweeted camp of gender multiplicity know, as unequivocally as the advocates of two genders, who and what they are, it seems that the winner of the tweet contest is the discourse of certainty itself, and that what is lost is the very idea of the *impossibility of knowing*. Indeed, there are critical trends in the academy that mirror the endorsement of knowing. The proponents of "Building a Better Description," the sequel to "Surface Reading," maintain that attentively drawn description avoids the pitfalls of suspicious critique.[14] And in the popular terrain of sex and gender politics, it does seem that the "surface" has won out on both the right and the left: that a feminist project that began as a critique of anatomical destiny more than three decades ago has closed with the rise of sex organs and the fall of critique.

But, again, the certainty conjured up in these agonistic

times has a particular flavor. In some cases, the flavor is fully fetishistic ("I know but all the same"); in other cases, it is a defiant staging of oppositions; but in both cases there is an expenditure of effort that belies the very meaning of *certainty*. It is not surprising that at this time there is a turn in the academy away from critique. The reasons for the turn range from an argument that critique probes too much, is too suspicious, to the complaint that it achieves too little, unable to tell us anything that we don't already know. Added to the anxious certainties, then, is a consensus that theoretical critical thinking, once so crucial, has lost its value. The problem is, to give up on trying to grasp the workings of sexuality is to give up on having any insight into its effects, into all the irrational violence and simple suffering unleased by the "obscenity of the unconscious." To be certain about sexuality—whether to master it through authoritarian dominance or to embrace it as one's personal truth—is to place one's stakes in a fantasy.

It is in the context of these symptomatic strains that I return to the old debate about how to theorize the impossibility of sexual difference. Far from being an outdated debate, it is deeply implicated in questions of knowing and not knowing, and hence in questions of critical reading. To look more closely at these implications I turn not to the feminist debates on sexual difference but to the impasse on the question that one finds in Derrida and Lacan. I do so because in the feminist debates the political possible inevitably complicates the theoretical impossible. With Derrida and Lacan, where the stakes are not political, *it is sexual difference that complicates reading*, putting into relief both the break between deconstructive and psychoanalytic modes of critique on the question of sexual difference, and the productive impossibility of critical reading today.

To turn to Derrida and Lacan is not, of course, to turn

away from feminist theory, at least from the type of theory that intersected with their work. So before revisiting the Derridean-Lacanian impasse, I offer a brief sketch of the historical connections between deconstruction and psychoanalysis on the one hand, and feminist theoretical challenges in the era of neoliberalism on the other.

2
Reading Sexual Difference

Feminist Intersections

Feminist theorists crossed paths with Derridean and Lacanian theories as the feminist politics that grew out of the anti-war and civil rights movements of the 1960s were channeled into at least three strong branches: the liberal branch fighting for women's social and political equality with men; the radical feminist branch seeking the overthrow of patriarchy in the service of gynocentrism; and the left branch that saw the male/female struggle as a symptom of racist capitalism, calling for systemic change in the name of social justice. Within academic feminism, the three modalities of liberal, radical, and left tended to intersect with various feminist challenges to existing disciplinary formations. Literary studies provided a rich terrain for liberal feminist explorations of character and authorship, for example; radical feminists could work in fields such as anthropology, religious studies, and the emerging field of lesbian studies; left inquiry blossomed in different ways in areas of women's history and in black feminist theory. There was one line of inquiry, however, for which there seemed to be no evident disciplinary space: the left criticism that looked to extend the boundaries of socialist and anti-racist feminisms to pursue questions of signification, epistemology, subjectivity, and so forth. Within the US academy there was no disciplinary space from which to pose certain foundational questions: what is a woman, what is a man, and what does it mean to ask those questions?

It was thus that some feminists, frustrated with the identitarian closure that tended to dominate feminist inquiry, turned to a range of theoretical modes of reading. The problem of closure is not an easy one to address, inscribed as it is in the very *ism* of feminism. How to escape from being the other of the masculine; how, in other words, to decenter androcentrism? To grasp the stakes these questions carried at the time, it is helpful to look at the editorial statements of *m/f*, a British journal published between 1978 and 1986. In the editors' words, *m/f* was "a project organized in the margins, outside any institutional support or constraint."[1] That project is summarized in the editorial introduction to the final issue:

> From the beginning we took certain concepts to
> be a problem and not a solution for feminism and
> we initiated a certain polemic with what had been
> understood as the first steps toward feminist theory
> at the time. As socialist-feminists we were opposed to
> the much discussed union of Marxism and feminism;
> on the other hand, committed as we were to the exploration of psychoanalytic theory, we did not think
> there could be any simple union of psychoanalysis
> and feminist theory. Above all, it seemed important
> to problematize the notion of sexual difference itself,

to suggest an analysis that went beyond the obvious division of "men" and "women."[2]

For *m/f*, the big theoretical-political challenge was to find a way out of the tautological structure of prevailing feminist thinking: "Our position has consistently been that there is and can be no *general* grounding of feminism, no essential femininity, no eternal forms of oppression and patriarchy. . . ."[3] It is not just that "women" can in no way be a unified term, as radical women of color and later intersectional theorists insisted, but that the very assumption of a unified term closes off the kinds of questions that might lead to political answers.[4] Instead of complexly intersecting discursive practices, one had structures that knew the answers in advance. And in place of questions, one had a series of positivities: men, patriarchy, oppression, domination. "If the outcome of this process were known in advance, the work *m/f* has demanded would not be necessary."

The difficulty for *m/f* was compounded by liberalism's notion of the unified subject. However important the category of the subject is for the liberal formulation of rights, it is rarely taken as the abstract category it is for liberalism, but rather as a commonsense descriptive term that affords unquestioned sense to notions such as "possession" (as in possession of one's body).[5] Moreover, and perhaps most problematic for *m/f*, was that the conventional categories of "men" and "women" require "full subjects already sexually differentiated, that is, organized into two unitary groups."[6] Hence *m/f*'s insistence on the psychoanalytic challenge to the fantasy of the fully organized sexual subject, an insistence that at the same time recognized the difficulty therein. The psychical and the social might be "inseparable" but not in any predictable way: "We suggest . . . that the psychical and the social do not meet as fully determinate domains whose relation is then one of causality, overdetermination or parallelism. Thus they cannot substitute for each other and they cannot have any necessary relation between them that can be stated in advance. To be concerned with sexual politics must necessitate tracing the *particular* forms of connection between psychical relations and social relations. . . ."[7]

However rich the theoretical-political project of *m/f*, by 1986 the editors determined that its moment had passed. Although they still recognized the need for a rigorous feminist discourse, the impediments to rigor seemed too great and their failures too apparent: "It can be said that where there was a measure of political agreement our theoretical effect has often been slight, and that where we have been theoretically welcome the political point has not always been sustained." Moreover, while the concerns evoked by the phrase "the personal is political" remained important, "'the personal' now seems to span a great complex and 'the political' seems a much more fragmented field."[8] For *m/f*, the effort to theorize feminist political thinking seemed increasingly futile. How to let air into the hermetically sealed narrative of patriarchal oppression that seemed so axiomatic? How to suggest that the "personal" was not in any simple way authorized by "experience"? How to counter the conviction that political energy was inevitably sapped by theoretical speculation?

The focus of *m/f* on the intersection of feminism, psychoanalysis, and Marxism, along with the challenges and frustrations the journal grappled with, were shared by US feminist theorists of the 1970s for whom deconstruction was also crucial. Gayatri Spivak, for example, never stopped insisting that the conjuncture demanded the arduous task of reading simultaneously as a Marxist, feminist, psychoanalytic, and deconstructive critic. The feminists of the "Yale

School"—notably Barbara Johnson and Shoshana Felman—were essential in theorizing the relationships between psychoanalytic and deconstructive readings.[9] And of course, the psychoanalytic-deconstructive connection was fundamental to theoretical developments in France from the 1960s on, including in "French feminism."

By the time *m/f* ceased publication in 1986, a new moment was emerging in US critical feminism, with historian Joan W. Scott's "Gender: A Useful Category of Historical Analysis" appearing that year and philosopher Judith Butler's *Gender Trouble: Feminism and the Subversion of Identity* four years later. With this development came a new problematic, namely an effort to destabilize received notions of sexuality through the analytic category of "gender." And although the theoretical project was different, the gender theorists embraced the challenges expressed by *m/f*, along with a theoretical commitment to both deconstruction and psychoanalysis.

What Derrida offered was a way out of the tautological closure of man/woman, the impossibility of woman's position as always already man's other. Take *"différance,"* for example. In dubbing as *différance* what Barbara Johnson calls "the lag inherent in any signifying act"—the lag inherent in language as a system of difference—Derrida exposes the metaphysical fantasy of the self-identical, the self-present. As Johnson glosses it, "to mean is automatically not to be."[10] And the feminist critic who read with an eye to *différance* was able to transform the self-certainty of the binary edifice of man/woman into the ever-moving reversals and displacements that so animate Western culture. In this way, in seeing *différance* at work, the feminist critic could see the power of the male principle: *not* an eternal oppressive power but one at once susceptible to the deconstructive collapse of its wily scaffolding *and*, at the same time, capable of erasing the collapse and re-erecting the unitary closure of what Derrida names phallogocentrism.

As for psychoanalysis, Lacan's return to Freud offered an escape from the humanist unified subject — a subject *always already* sexually bifurcated and programmed for heterosexual reproduction. Psychoanalysis learns from the unconscious, the logic of which is totally different from conscious logic; it attends not to instinctual development but to the work of the drives; and it looks neither to anatomy nor to physiology to explain the operations of the psyche. Rather than taking the human subject as a given, psychoanalysis asks *how* the subject comes about, and sees it constituted in division, that is, in a break that symbolization entails in the field of alterity — the field of the Other. As Lacan says, it is in the unconscious that one sees the effects of speech on the subject. And when psychoanalysis asks how sexually differentiated subjects come about, the answer is: with great difficulty. For the sexual division — the radical fissure — appears in the symbolic order not as unsignifiable — but as *prohibition* — what Lacan calls the paternal metaphor. And it is in relation to that seeming prohibition that subjects take on their sexual positions. Something they never fully succeed in doing — which gives feminism room to breathe.

Derridean and Lacanian Crossings

At first glance, the Derridean and Lacanian positions could be seen to correspond to the tweet Rose cites:[11] "If you want a country with 63 genders vote Clinton; if you want a country where men are men and women are women vote Trump." Indeed, in "Choreographies," Derrida declares he would like "to believe in the multiplicity of sexually marked voices," of "a relationship to the other where the code of sexual marks would no longer be discriminating": "The relationship would not be a-sexual, far from it, but would be sexual otherwise: beyond the binary difference that governs the decorum of all codes, beyond the opposition masculine/feminine, beyond bisexuality as well, beyond homosexuality and heterosexuality which come to the same thing."[12] By contrast, in *Encore*, Lacan divides his sexuation diagram into left and right: "Every speaking being situates itself on one side or the other. On the left, the lower line . . . indicates that it is through the phallic function that man as a whole acquires his inscription"; "On the other side, you have the inscription for the woman portion of speaking beings."[13]

Of course, neither Derrida nor Lacan is addressing questions of gender. Derrida's multiplicity would be as unrecognizable to the tweet's author as Lacan's two. That shared similarity — the theoretical challenges both Derrida and Lacan pose to commonsense understandings of sexuality and subjectivity — does explain in part how two theorists on such radically opposed sides of the differences/difference divide both informed feminist critique. Nor were feminists alone in their embrace of the two. Elisabeth Roudinesco describes the enthusiasm of Phillipe Sollers and others at *Tel Quel*:

> In 1966, *Tel Quel* published Jacques Derrida's paper "Freud and the Scene of Writing." From the perspective of a surfacing of the "trace," Lacan's reelaboration also aroused a great deal of interest, and particularly his theory of the division of the subject. Through it, the writers of *Tel Quel* could become Freudians; they read Freud in the light of Lacan, Lacan under the banner of Derrida, and Derrida according to a guerrilla-like strategy of the written. It mattered little that those endeavors were opposed to one another; they seemed to be speaking the same language: signifiers, texts, and inscriptions.[14]

That Freud could be read through Lacan, Lacan through Derrida, and Derrida through the battle cry of *écriture* had as much to do with the explosion of theoretical work in the 1960s as with a lack of critical discernment. As François Dosse comments in his *History of Structuralism*, the mid-1960s was a time when "the apprentice structuralist reader had to read constantly."[15] Consider the publications of Derrida and Lacan in the three-year period 1965–1968: Derrida's "De la grammatologie" in *Critique*, 1965; his "Freud et la scène de l'écriture" in *Tel Quel*, 1966; Lacan's nine hundred-page *Écrits* with Seuil, 1966; in 1967, Derrida's *De la grammatologie* with Minuit, *L'Écriture et la différence* with Seuil, and *La Voix et le phénomène* with PUF; and in 1968, Derrida's "Différance" in *Tel Quel*. Finally in October, 1966, both gave papers at the Johns Hopkins Symposium on "The Language of Criticism and the Sciences of Man": Derrida his "Structure, Sign and Play in the Discourse of the Human Sciences," and Lacan his "Of Structure as an Inmixing of an Otherness Prerequisite to Any Subject Whatever."[16]

If the lines between Derrida and Lacan were blurred in the 1960s, more than a half-century ago, what can be said of today — some fifty years since French theoretical excitement hit the US and at least two decades since US academic interest in that form of theoretical critique began to collapse? It is thus that I revisit in some detail a set of theoretical questions that will strike some readers as common knowledge. I do so because it is when one looks closely at the two theoretical discourses that the Derridean-Lacanian split over sexual difference — which Derrida vigorously asserts in "Le Facteur de la vérité" and elsewhere — both does and does not make sense.[17] That is, the investments of the two theorists coincide in so many respects that one could imagine Derrida reading Lacan differently. But that is not the case.

A close look at the Derridean-Lacanian connections reveals that the split between the two has to do primarily with their reading strategies. For all the differences between the philosopher and the psychoanalyst, the most fundamental difference is how they read, not only how they read Freud, other texts, and each other, but the very critical stances from which they read. The split is particularly significant in that the two share the understanding of reading that drives the theoretical work of the 1960s: reading not as decoding or hermeneutic interpretation but as a practice attentive to the ways language works in the breakdown of its representational powers. In their readings of sexual difference, then, both Derrida and Lacan shed light on the complex knot of reading, meaning, and sexuality. But in reading the impossibility differently, they show there is more than one such knot.

Although Derrida and Lacan seem at times to be speaking the same generalized language of their period, their critical projects involve different problematics. Derrida's is philosophical and the limits he challenges are those of the Western philosophical tradition. Yet, to say the limits are philosophical is not to say they are parochial. As Johnson comments, when Derrida undertakes a critique of "Western metaphysics," he means not only the philosophical tradition "but 'everyday' thought and language as well."[18] In his "Letter to a Japanese Friend," in which Derrida elaborates the meanings of "deconstruction," he indicates how fundamental the critique is: "one of the principal things at stake in what is called in the texts 'deconstruction' is precisely the delimiting of onto-logic and above all the third-person present indicative: S *is* P."[19] In challenging the very logic of ontology, Derrida challenges metaphysics *tout court*: the delimited *is* continues to signify, of course, but without the grounding of self-identical originary presence on which metaphysics stands. Derrida's *is* reminds philosophy that there is no thought without language and that in language the trace obviates the closure of origin and essence. It is Derrida's theorization of the trace that troubles metaphysical presence: "The trace is not a presence but is rather the simulacrum of presence that dislocates, displaces, and refers beyond itself."[20]

If the trace is the "always already" absent presence, the neologism *différance* involves the play of the trace, the play of the differences and deferrals that make up meaning. It is this play that philosophy has repressed, Derrida argues, and this repression that he is determined to undo, not through the speculative theorizing of philosophy but through a reading practice that looks rigorously at the ways a text controls and *fails* to control its own deconstruction. The drama in a Derridean reading is always immanent to the text, its register that of language rather than that of the reading-writing subject. And language has its own play of grammatical voices. Whereas an infinitive like *différer* indicates an activity, Derrida comments, the *ance* of *différance* neutralizes the simply active: ". . . that which lets itself be designated *différance* is neither simply active nor simply passive, announcing or rather recalling something like the middle voice, saying an operation that is not an operation, an operation that cannot be conceived either as a passion or as the action of a subject on an object. . . . For the middle voice might be what philosophy, at its outset, distributed into an active and a passive voice, thereby constituting itself by means of this repression."[21]

What the repression produces, for Derrida, is the architechtonic grounding of metaphysics in presence without trace, as in the divine logos of Greek cosmology and the Word of Christian ontotheology. And if logocentrism guarantees the self-presence of a generalized ontology, phallocentrism names the active principle at work in philosophical logic: the original phallic One. Yet, no matter how vigorously philosophical thought shores up its edifice, the work of *différance* cannot be contained, just as meaning cannot be nailed down. What is involved for Derrida is not polysemia, not the possible multiple meanings of a sign, but what any given meaning necessarily leaves out or subordinates. It is the *"remainder* irreducible to the dominant force which organized the — to say it quickly — logocentric hierarchy."[22]

The overturning and displacement of this hierarchy is what Derrida calls "dissemination." In Johnson's words, "dissemination" is "what subverts . . . recuperative gestures of mastery. It is what foils the attempt to progress in an orderly way toward meaning or knowledge, what breaks the circuit of intentions or expectations through some ungovernable excess or loss.[23]" It is not surprising then that Derridean dissemination has such a feminine flavor, and not only in the overturning of the sexual binary. In Derrida's readings, the unruly feminine — so prevalent a trope in Western formulations of man/woman — continually subverts phallic origin and mastery, not as an oppositional force but as *constitutive* — always-already.

Of course, the Derridean woman *is* not. With Derrida's woman we move, as Johnson says in another context, from the ontological to the undecidable. In *Spur's: Nietzsche's Styles*, woman's unstable positions as truth, as untruth, undo the possibility of a coherent hermeneutic message. Again, the feminine undecidable is the subversion of the ontological. In "The Double Session," for example, the crucial figure of the hymen derives its undecidability not just from its meanings (membrane and Greek god of marriage), but from its syntactical position in texts of Plato and Mallarmé that engage mimesis (along with beds and conjugal sheets . . .). It is the textual play on the homonym *antre* (cave) and *entre* (between) that stages the undecidability: "It [the hymen] produces its effect first and foremost through the syntax, which disposes the 'entre' in such a way that the suspense is due only to the placement and not to the context of the words.... It is the 'between' whether it names fusion or separation, that thus carries all the force of the operation. The hymen must be determined through the *entre* and not the other way around."[24]

And it is in the context of (feminine) undecidability that we can see the "multiplicity of sexually marked voices" that Derrida calls for in "Choreographies" as a very particular form of dissemination: "beyond the binary difference that governs the decorum of all codes, beyond the opposition masculine/feminine, beyond bisexuality as well, beyond homosexuality and heterosexuality...."[25] What is at issue is not multiplication but the movement of displacement. Derrida underlines the problem with thinking in terms of the binary:

> [W]hen sexual difference is determined by *opposition* in the dialectical sense ... one appears to set off "the war between the sexes"; but one precipitates the end with victory going to the masculine sex. The determination of sexual difference in opposition is destined, designed, in truth, for truth; it is so in order to erase sexual difference. The dialectical opposition neutralizes or supersedes [Hegel's term *Aufhebung* carries with it both the sense of conserving and negating ...] the difference. However, according to a surreptitious operation that must be flushed out, one insures the phallocentric mastery under the cover of neutralization every time. These are now well known paradoxes.[26]

Hence the importance of displacement, evoked in "Choreographies" through the figure of the dance. The sexual multiplicity at stake is the "multiplicity of places, moments, forms and forces. . . . How can one breathe without such punctuation and without the multiplication of rhythm and steps?"[27]

"Choreographies" is a dialogue between Derrida and Christie McDonald in which Derrida elaborates his views on feminism by inviting McDonald and the reader to meditate on the connections, in Anne Berger's words, among "dance, differance, reading, and sexual difference."[28] What we learn, Berger writes, is that Derrida's sexual difference has to do with "sexing differances." In other words, sexual multiplicity for Derrida has to do with language, that is to say, with reading, something Berger makes explicit: "Sexual difference(s), for Derrida, do not give themselves to see; they are not a question of perception, much less of evidence, nor even of fantasy. They lend themselves to reading and to reading only."[29]

Of course, for Derrida "reading only" does not mean "only reading." As with the deconstructed *is*, everything is at stake for Derrida in the work of undoing the stranglehold of metaphysical closure. In his last interview, with Jean Birnbaum in *Le Monde*, Derrida's insistence on "survival"—"la survie"—draws together language and life itself. The meaning of survival, he says, "is not to be added on to living and dying: life *is* living on, life is survival [la vie *est* survie]." He goes on: "All the concepts that have helped me in my work, and notably that of the trace or of the spectral were related to this 'surviving' as a structural and originary dimension. It is not derived from either living or dying. No more than what I call 'originary mourning, that is, a mourning that does not wait for the so-called 'actual' death."[30] And near the end of the interview: ". . . survival is an originary concept that constitutes the very structure of what we call existence, Dasein, if you will. . . . Everything I say . . . about survival as a complication of the opposition life/death proceeds in me from an unconditional affirmation of life."[31]

As the *Tel Quel* of 1966 attests, the sharp divide between Derrida and Lacan can be obscured by all that seems to bind them: critique of presence and of origin, centrality of language and signification, critique of interiority and the classical subject, importance of repetition, and so forth. In a talk on Lacan and Derrida, the psychoanalyst Frida Saal observes that the two names should be joined by a rhomboid or diamond—the symbol that both joins and separates: "in the relationship/non-relationship that is established [between] them, a tension is created that implies simultaneously a union and a disjunction, in the perspective of a theoretical encounter that is at the same time necessary and impossible."[32] Here I can only indicate with a broad brush some of the crossings that contribute to their deadlock regarding sexual difference.

Consider the two theorists' approaches to the question of the subject. Philosopher Derrida seeks early on to deconstruct the self-presence of the sovereign subject in his critique of Edmund Husserl's theorization of a phenomenological "now."[33] In doing so, he displaces the classical subject onto what David Roden calls a "scriptural subjectivity" based on the logic of the trace, a "quasi-transcendental ... not exclusive to the structure of human consciousness or awareness."[34] The Derridean trace has no secondary relation to the full-presence of the logos, no relationship to origin. It is what Derrida calls the very presence-absence of the movement of signification, a movement that is foreclosed by the category of the sovereign subject.[35]

If Derrida the philosopher displaces the subject, Lacan *introduces* a retheorized subject into psychoanalytic discourse.[36] The main attraction for Lacan is the linguistic subject, which allows him to incorporate structural linguistics into psychoanalytic thinking. Both theorists invest in language, then, the one by ridding himself of the subject, the other radically retheorizing it. While Derrida supplants the classical subject with the cunning ruses of signification that never fail to undermine fantasies of conscious control, Lacan finds in language the very ruses that Freud had discovered in the unconscious and sees the subject precisely *as their effect*. Lacan's subject is, indeed, the subject of the unconscious, produced by the Symbolic order. Unlike the ego or "I," which Lacan views as produced in the register of the Imaginary, the subject emerges from the Symbolic order, that register of shared socio-linguistic structures and significations, of radical alterity, or in Lacan's terminology, the Other.[37] Thrown into the Symbolic, the subject is born: "an effect of language," Lacan writes, "in that he is born of this early split."[38] Or, as Andrew Lewis writes, "It is not that the subject is split but that the subject *is this splitting*."[39]

The Lacanian subject of the unconscious is "nothing other than what slides in a chain of signifiers."[40] What Lacan draws on especially is the Saussurean understanding of language as a closed system of differential elements. While borrowing from Saussure, however, Lacan takes only what suits his analytic understanding of the unconscious. For Saussure, the basic unit of language is the sign, composed of the phonological signifier and the conceptual signified. For Lacan, what constitutes the play of the unconscious most importantly is the signifier: "The unconscious is fundamentally structured, woven, chained, meshed, by language. And not only does the signifier play as big a role there as the signified does, but it plays the fundamental role." He goes on to say, "the relationship between signifier and signified is far from being, as they say in set theory, one-to-one."[41]

Early in *On Grammatology*, Derrida inserts a footnote

that inaugurates what will be numerous repeated sharp criticisms of the notion of the primacy of the signifier. Although Lacan is not mentioned by name, in 1967 the reference is clear. Derrida finds the "primacy" of the signifier an "untenable and absurd" expression, impossible to state "without putting the very idea of the sign into suspicion."[42] Of course, putting the sign into suspicion is just what Lacan wants to do. Like Derrida, he undermines the sign, but in different ways and for different reasons. And it is not just the sign he warns against but the signified. For Lacan, the importance of the Saussurean formulation is the cut that marks the separation of signifier and signified, to say nothing of that between the sign and referent:

> The trap, the hole one must not fall into, is the belief that signifieds are objects, things. The signified is something quite different . . . it always refers to meaning, that is, to another meaning, The system of language, at whatever point you take ahold of it, never results in an index finger directly indicating a point of reality; it's the whole of reality that is covered by the entire network of language.[43]

The question of unconscious meaning, then, is never a one-to-one matter. The analyst who learns from the unconscious looks not to what a sign points to ("where there's smoke there's fire"), but to the way the subject slides in the network of signifiers. As Lacan writes: "It [the unconscious] speaks in the Other, I say, designating by 'Other' the very locus evoked by recourse to speech in any relation in which such recourse plays a part. If it speaks in the Other, whether or not the subject hears it with his ear, it is because it is there that the subject finds his signifying place in a way that is logically prior to any awakening of the signified."[44] This is why Freud never fully solves the enigma of a dream, never fully closes an analysis, but finds insights in the chains of associations.[45]

What further separates Lacan's psychoanalytic problematic from the philosophical problematic of Derrida, what drives their split over sexual difference is, of course, Lacan's engagement with Freudian *sexuality* and its tie to the unconscious. Freud transformed the notion of human sexuality by conceiving of the drive (*Trieb*) as "lying on the frontier between the mental and the physical." As such, it deviates constitutively from the biological, pursuing its own satisfaction.[46] But as Alenka Zupančič explains, we learn from Freud (no stranger to the logic of the supplement) that what is at issue is no simple deviation or derivation:

> . . . in human beings, all satisfaction of a need allows, in principle, for another satisfaction to occur, which tends to become independent and self-perpetuating in pursuing and reproducing itself. There is no natural need that would be absolutely pure, i.e. devoid of the surplus element that splits it from within. This split, this interval of void, this original non-convergence of two different versants of satisfaction is, for Freud, the very site or ground of human sexuality.[47]

By recasting Freud through the signifier and the subject-as-splitting, Lacan thus foregrounds sexuality as this short-circuiting of the vital and psychical orders. But again, one must insist on the radicality of Freud's insight. What is at stake is not a straightforward break between the vital and the psychical, not the (metaphysical) pathos of the mind/body split. The dislocation of the two is due not, Zupančič writes, to "their heterogeneous origins (for example, that one comes from the body and the other from the symbolic order), but on the contrary to the fact that they *originate at the same place*."⁴⁸ Thus is sexuality constitutively out of joint, split by an originary non-convergence of vital need and psychic satisfaction.

It is because of the constitutive deviation of the drives that Freud sees sexuality at work in the highest accomplishments of human culture. Zupančič continues: "The generative source of culture is sexual in this precise sense of belonging to the supplementary satisfaction that serves no immediate function and satisfies no immediate need."⁴⁹ It is not, then, that Freud locates sex in bodily organs as well as "all over the place:" "His claim was that sex is lacking from its home, that its 'home' was the one place where sex is not to be found. . . . It starts as a secondary, surplus, collateral satisfaction produced in the process of satisfaction of bodily needs. . . . This essentially collateral surplus satisfaction is what he conceptualized as the drive."⁵⁰

For Lacan, the power of the drives is played out in desire, which emerges as a surplus factor in the child's demand to have its vital needs met: "Desire begins to take shape in the margin in which demand rips away from need, Lacan writes."⁵¹ And in "The Signification of the Phallus":

Demand in itself bears on something other than the satisfaction it calls for. It is demand for a presence or an absence. This is what the primordial relationship with the mother manifests, replete as it is with that Other who must be situated *shy of* needs that the Other can fulfill. . . . In this way, demand annuls (*aufhebt*) the particularity of everything that can be granted, by transmuting it into a proof of love, and the very satisfactions demand obtains for need are debased (*sich erniedrigt*) to the point of being no more than the crushing brought on by the demand for love. . . .⁵²

Lacan goes on to write that "the particularity thus abolished reappear(s) *beyond* demand" and "the power of pure loss emerges from the residue of an obliteration.... This is why desire is neither the appetite for satisfaction nor the demand for love, but the difference that results from the subtraction of the first from the second, the very phenomenon of their splitting (Spaltung)."

The signifier of this splitting for Lacan is the phallus. It is thus that "[t]he phallus is the privileged signifier of this mark in which the role [*part*] of Logos is wedded to the advent of desire."[53] Its function — the phallic function — is the castration that institutes the subject in the field of the Other in which the subject's alienated needs come back in the form of desire. For Lacan, the interruption of the mother-child dyad takes the form of a prohibition. Jacqueline Rose writes:

> By breaking the imaginary dyad, the phallus represents a moment of division (Lacan calls this the subject's "lack-in-being") which reenacts the fundamental splitting of subjectivity itself. And by jarring against any naturalist account of sexuality ... the phallus regulates sexuality to a strictly other dimension — the order of the symbolic outside of which, for Lacan, sexuality cannot be understood. The importance of the phallus is that its status in the development of human sexuality is something which nature *cannot* account for.[54]

It is not nature that accounts for the phallus but the androcentric symbolic, which means, Rose writes: "For Lacan men and women are only ever in language.... All speaking beings must line themselves up on one side or the other of this division, but anyone can cross over and inscribe themselves on the opposite side from that to which they are anatomically destined."[55] Having or not having a penis does not determine sexuation, however much reason and common sense dictate the reverse. It is not that anatomical difference *is* sexual difference, "but that anatomical difference comes to *figure* sexual difference, that is, it becomes the sole representative of what that difference is allowed to be."[56]

The problem, Lacan writes, is that the enigma produced by the gap of subtraction—subtraction of the satisfaction of needs from the demand for love—governs the closed field of desire in which "for each of the partners in the relationship, both the subject and the Other, it is not enough to be subjects of need or objects of love—they must hold the place of the cause of desire."[57] This lies at the heart of all the problems of sexual life, Lacan says. No matter what efforts to cover over the gap, the subject cannot achieve wholeness, "once the play of displacement and condensation to which he is destined in the exercise of his functions marks his relation, as a subject, to the signifier."[58]

The difference between the masculine and feminine positions in the sexed subject's splitting has to do with the subject's position vis-à-vis the Other and the kind of jouissance obtained. In *Encore*, Lacan distinguishes between the phallic *jouissance* of the masculine position and the Other jouissance of the feminine. In the famous sexuation formula, he borrows from symbolic logic to evoke the asymmetrical positions of male and female jouissance. The logic of phallic jouissance is of a finite structure: the masculine position is "wholly" subject to the phallic function of alienation in the Symbolic. But, as is the case with finite logic, the law of the universal whole depends on the exception, the one not subjected to the Law (as in the Freudian fantasy of the primal father). Deploying the fantasy of the exception available to the male subject, Lacan is able then to suggest the power of the phallus in the androcentric register of the Symbolic *and* its fraudulence.

In contrast is the logic of the infinite that he employs to figure feminine *jouissance*. It is not that the feminine subject is not subject to the phallic function; all speaking subjects are castrated. It is that in the logic of the phallic function, Woman (la *femme*) is not subject to the fantasized universal whole. The feminine position is the not-whole, the not-all; la *femme*, subject to phallic signification, may be said not to exist. But there is something more, Lacan says. There is a *jouissance* beyond the phallus: "There is a jouissance that is hers (*à elle*), that belongs to that 'she' (*elle*) that doesn't exist and doesn't signify anything."[59]

In the first segment (titled "I always speak the truth") of a staged televised interview aired during the year of the twentieth Seminar, *Encore*, Lacan begins with these words: "I always speak the truth. Not the whole truth, because there's no way to say it all. Saying it all is literally impossible. Words fail."[60] In a later segment (titled "Knowing, doing, hoping"), he says that woman enters into the masquerade of femininity, preparing herself "on-the-off-chance, so that her inner fantasy of Man will find its hour of truth. That's not excessive, since truth is already woman insofar as it's not-all, unable, in any case, to be wholly-spoken."[61]

As for Derrida, in "Le Facteur de la vérité," his reading of Lacan's "Seminar on 'The Purloined Letter,'" he draws a sharp line between deconstruction and Lacanian theory, a line that cuts right through the question of woman-as-truth. What is fraudulent, Derrida argues, is the very theory of phallic fraudulence and the truth born by woman. For Derrida, to the contrary, the truth that Lacan delivers is nothing other than phallogocentrism at its purest.

The Break

In "Différance" and elsewhere, Derrida expresses his debt to (or, as he writes in *Archive Fever*, his "inheritance of") Freud's theorizing of the trace and the logic of the unconscious. At question in these readings is always a tension Derrida finds between Freud's radical challenge to metaphysics on the one hand—a challenge that so enables deconstruction—and what he perceives as Freud's indebtedness to metaphysics on the other.

Derrida's engagement with Lacan is something quite different. In Peggy Kamuf's words, "'Le Facteur de la vérité' constitutes Derrida's patient reply to those who are in a hurry to assimilate deconstruction to Lacanian psychoanalytic theory."[62] With due respect to Kamuf, "patience" does not seem to capture the uncensored agonism of Derrida's critique of the "Seminar on 'The Purloined Letter.'" It is not undecidability that drives this reading but reversal—a straightforward effort to rectify what Derrida considers a theoretical travesty.

In reading Poe's tale of the effects a purloined letter has on a series of people (including among others the Queen, the King and a conniving minister), Lacan makes of the letter what Johnson calls "a kind of allegory of the signifier,"[63] aiming to evoke how the human being "manifests its capture" in the symbolic chain: "Which is why we have decided to illustrate for you today," Lacan writes, "the truth which may be drawn from that moment in Freud's thought under study—namely, that it is the symbolic order which is constitutive for the subject—by demonstrating in a story the decisive orientation which the subject receives from the itinerary of a signifier."[64]

Early on in "Le Facteur de la vérité," Derrida cites the ways Lacan presents the letter/signifier as theoretically audacious: in Lacan's view, its effect depends not on its content, not on any "naïve semanticism" but on its circulation. Similarly, it seems to have no proper place, no ideal place, as Lacan asserts in a passage cited by Derrida: "For the signifier is a unit in its very uniqueness, being by nature symbol only of an absence. Which is why," Lacan writes, "we cannot say of the purloined letter that, like other objects, it must be *or* not be in a particular place but unlike them it will be and not be where it is, wherever it goes."[65]

These claims fail to persuade Derrida. A theoretically audacious letter-signifier is emphatically *not* what he finds in the "Seminar on 'The Purloined Letter.'" Indeed, Derrida's estimation of Lacan's reading could not be more disparaging: "From the beginning we recognize the classical landscape of applied psychoanalysis. It is applied in this case to literature. The status of Poe's text is never challenged — Lacan simply calls it 'fiction' — yet, Poe's text is summoned up as an example. It is an example for the sake of 'illustrating' through a dialectical process a law and a truth which form the proper object of the Seminar."[66]

Derrida charges Lacan with drawing an arbitrary frame around a segment of Poe's story in order to illustrate a psychoanalytic truth — the truth about castration. Or, as he writes in the opening lines of his essay, "it is psychoanalysis itself, supposedly, that finds itself" (*"La psychanalyse, à supposer, se trouve."*)[67] What Derrida considers most unacceptable is Lacan's figuration of the phallus as a signifier with no signified, a signifier that marks the lack-in-being (*le manque-à-être*) that for Lacan figures the subject's constitutive split into language. For Derrida, the fraudulence of the phallus — its dead giveaway, as it were — derives from the centrality of speech in psychoanalysis:

> If "the phallus is the privileged signifier of this mark where the share of the logos [*la part du logos*] is conjoined to the advent of desire" . . . the privileged locus of this privileged signifier, its letter then, is the voice: the spokesman [*porte-parole*]. It alone admits, as soon as the point of stability of the signified assures

it its repeatable identity, the ideality or the idealization power necessary to safeguard . . . the indivisible, unique, non-mutilable integrity of the phallus. . . . The *transcendental* position of the phallus . . . would thus have its proper locus . . . in the phonemic structure of language.[68]

Far from a signifier without a signified, Derrida reads the Lacanian phallus as "phallogocentristic transcendentalism," a reading he forecasts early in his essay by wittily turning *"manque à sa place"* (the lack always missing from its place) into *"manque a sa place"* (lack *has* its place).[69] For Derrida, it is clear that in figuring castration as the place of lack, the place in the symbolic order where the signifier marks lack-in-being, Lacan's whole theoretical edifice reproduces the most traditional metaphysical notions of presence and absence, with woman as the truth of castration. And in Derrida's view, "The Seminar on 'The Purloined Letter'" simply repeats this edifice:

By determining the place of the lack (the topos of what is missing from its place), by constituting it as a fixed center, Lacan is in fact proposing at once a discourse-truth and a discourse on the truth of the purloined letter as the truth of "The Purloined Letter." In spite of the appearance of denegation, his is a hermeneutical decipherment. The link between Femininity and Truth is its ultimate signified."[70]

Derrida supports this reading with ample footnotes to other writings of Lacan as well as of Freud, Melanie Klein, and others. Moreover, he incorporates in his reading Marie Bonaparte's analysis of the Poe story in which the stolen letter is found hanging from a clitoris-like knob over a fireplace, and once returned to the Queen, represents her missing penis. All this he presents as evidence, in spite of the fact that neither Bonaparte, nor castration, let alone the penis, are named in Lacan's text. It is ironic, then, that Derrida follows his criticism of Lacan's "undisinterested" framing of the argument with a declaration of his own interest: "Something is missing from its place but the lack itself is never missing. Because of castration, the phallus always remains in place in the transcendental topology we spoke of above.... The difference I am interested in here is that the lack has no place in dissemination — a formula to be understood however you will."[71]

Although it is not surprising to encounter in Derrida's essay a contest pitting dissemination against the phallus, it is curious to see a reader normally so attentive to the scene of writing mount an argument so indebted to extra-textual materials. In "The Frame of Reference: Poe, Lacan, Derrida," Barbara Johnson exposes the ways Derrida's and Lacan's writings meet and miss each other, and how Derrida's reading of "The Seminar" repeats the crimes of which he accuses Lacan. How "one-upmanship" inevitably turns into "one-downmanship," is, she says, "the very logic of the purloined letter."[72]

While Johnson goes on to show the ways Derrida's and Lacan's essays are both implicated in this logic, there are moments where she explicitly acknowledges her evident puzzlement at Derrida's reading.[73] One of these moments is where Derrida responds to Lacan's final statement of the formula whereby "the sender, we tell you, receives from the receiver his own message in reverse form. Thus it is that what the 'purloined letter,' nay, the 'letter in suffrance,' means is that a letter always arrives at its destination."[74] Taking this as yet another instance of the phallogocentric suppression of *différance*, Derrida retorts: "Dissemination mutilates the unity of the signifier, that is, of the phallus."[75]

Unconvinced, Johnson turns to Lacan's text. Reading the contested section in context, she shows how a series of reversals and ambiguities in his text "seem sufficient to problematize, if not subvert, the presupposition of univocality that is the very foundation on which Derrida has edified his interpretation." She continues with the following, which I cite at length in that it is so unwonted:

> But surely such an oversimplification on Derrida's part does not result from mere blindness, oversight, or error. . . . Derrida being the sharp-eyed reader that he is, his consistent forcing of Lacan's statements into systems and patterns from which they are actually trying to escape must correspond to some strategic necessity different from the attentiveness to the letter of the text which characterizes Derrida's ways of reading Poe. And, in fact, the more one works with Derrida's analysis, the more convinced one becomes that although the critique of what Derrida calls psychoanalysis is entirely justified, it does not quite apply to what Lacan's text is actually saying. Derrida argues, in effect, not against Lacan's *text* but against Lacan's *power*—or rather, against "Lac," as the apparent cause of certain effects of power in French discourse today. Whatever Lacan's text may *say*, it functions, according to Derrida, as if it said what *he* says it says."[76]

However valid Johnson's speculation, there may be another way to account for Derrida's striking failure to address what Lacan is really saying. Derrida's flat, literal readings not only ironically *highlight* Lacan's statements about the literality of the signifier; they also call for what Althusser terms a symptomatic reading. For Althusser, the symptomatic reading can reveal the textual effects of the meeting of incompatible *problematics*. An example Althusser uses in *Reading Capital* is the encounter of Marx and the classical political economists, an encounter commonly understood as the *same* object (the value of labor) addressed by two different methods, with Marx's method correcting and completing what preceded. In Althusser's terms, such a view misconstrues the encounter because it views it as historicist, that is, situated in a linear and continuous time that affords different perspectives on an object that is similarly continuous. Althusser argues, to the contrary, that Marx's text represents a radical break with historicism in that it formulates an entirely different object. The different object that Marx produces is the labor theory of value, produced within a problematic incommensurate with that of classical political economy.[77]

In Derrida's case, one could say that the incommensurability of his problematic and Lacan's renders it impossible for him to encounter Lacan on Lacan's terms. Nonetheless, from the beginning, critics were eager to assimilate Derridean and Lacanian theories. In a 1971 interview with Derrida, Jean-Louis Houdebine asks, for example: "what relationship does a problematic of writing seem to you to maintain to the problematic of the signifier such as Lacan has developed it, in which the signifier 'represents the subject for another signifier'?"[78] In response, in a long footnote attached to the interview, Derrida undertakes his first sustained critique of Lacan.[79] With "Le Facteur de la vérité" several years later, his frustration with what he considers the desire to collapse radically different work becomes fully visible.[80]

The incommensurability of Derrida and Lacan is evident in their very different views on the question of the psychic subject. As Rose writes in 1986, Derrida sees it as "a vestige of the logocentrism of the West."[81] And when Elisabeth Roudinesco asks Derrida in her 2004 dialogue with him why he avoids Freud's major metapsychological writings, preferring marginal and speculative texts, Derrida says explicitly that he looks to Freud not for his theories of the psychic subject but for what contributes to his own thinking: "my concern was to find, in a 'logic of the unconscious' (but I never made this expression my own), something with which to support a discourse that, from another place . . . I felt to be necessary." Hence, he drew from Freud "motifs of deferred action, delay, or 'originary' differance, everything that ruined or threatened the absolute phenomenological authority of the 'living present'. . . ." This, he says, is his positive gesture, the other being his vigilance against the metaphysical elements at work in Freud and Lacan.[82]

In perhaps her most probing intervention, Roudinesco responds by reminding Derrida of the theoretical reach of Freud's metapsychology, suggesting that it might have a certain relevance to his own concerns:

> Freud saw in what he called metapsychology a way to take psychoanalysis out of psychology and to prevent it from being subservient to philosophy. Unable to bring psychoanalysis into the natural sciences, he invented metapsychology, that is, a speculative model in order to inscribe it in the intersection of the natural sciences and speculative reflection. Hence the idea of translating metaphysics into a metapsychology, that is, of renouncing the knowledge of being for that of the unconscious.[83]

In response, Derrida grants that it was no doubt necessary to break with psychology but that he does not believe Freud's conceptual apparatus will last much longer:

> I may be mistaken, but the id, the ego, the superego, the ego ideal, the secondary process and the primary process of repression, etc. — in a word, the

> large Freudian machines (including the concept and the word "unconscious") — are in my opinion only provisional weapons, or even rhetorical tools cobbled together to be used against a philosophy of consciousness, of transparent and fully responsible intentionality.... I do not think that a metapsychology can hold up for long under scrutiny. Already, it is hardly being talked about anymore.[84]

Of course, Derrida's blunt dismissal of the psychic apparatus in no way lessens his deep interest in psychoanalysis, an interest he pursues over numerous volumes. Nowhere is this interest more intriguing than in *The Postcard: From Socrates to Freud and Beyond*, where he elaborates what he calls the postal principle, that structure of classical ontology in which all differences circulate back to the same, to the One. Although in "Le Facteur de la vérité" he sees the signifier/phallus as unequivocally subsumed by the postal principle, the question is more complex with the Freudian PP of *Beyond the Pleasure Principle*. There, in "To Speculate — on 'Freud'," Derrida mobilizes the tension in the Freudian text between the postal principle and dissemination, and the overlap or crossing of Freudian and Heideggerian speculations.[85]

However, for all of Derrida's dispersal of the subject across the scene of writing, for all the mutilation of identity by dissemination, Rose observes that identity returns for Derrida in *The Postcard*: ". . . identity returns in Derrida through the category of mastery as the metaconceptual and transcendent drive, so that something in the order of a psychic exigency seems to underpin the logos itself. Behind the Western logos of presence, Derrida locates an archi-trace or *différance* which that logos would ideally forget, but this then requires a psychic account of how/why that forgetting takes place."[86]

The undeniable force Derrida finds in phallogocentrism, the force he names the "drive of the proper" is captured in *The Postcard* in a flourish of rhetorical tautology: "the most driven drive is the drive of the proper, in other words, the one that tends to reappropriate itself. The movement of reappropriation is the most driven drive."[87]

As for what drives Derrida, he suggests in an intervention in 1979 that "Necessity is the Drive":

I often ask myself the question — "Why, why insist on deconstructing something which is so good?" And the only answer I have is that there is something that contradicts in ourselves or in myself the desire for this good. But where does this contradiction come from? First, I give it a name, which I sometimes write with a capital letter, that is, Necessity. And I write this word with a capital letter just to emphasize that it's a singular — Necessity, as a personal, as a single person. I have to do with Necessity itself, that is, something or someone, some *x*, which compels me to admit that my desire for good, for presence, my own metaphysics of presence, not only cannot be accomplished, meets its limit, but should not be accomplished — because the accomplishment or the fulfillment of this desire for presence would be Death itself.[88]

How appropriate that the Necessity that drives Derrida is personified. How better to evoke a psychic force underpinning phallogocentrism for Derrida. As Derrida attests often, his work is intensely personal, so much so that in his final interview he movingly reaffirms how all of the theoretical concepts that helped him in his work are related to "survival" as an originary concept of the structure of existence. With Necessity appearing here "as a personal, as a single person," compelling him to abandon his desire for presence, "scriptural subjectivity" takes on a decidedly transferential dimension.

Derrida's complex relationship to psychoanalysis indeed further complicates any effort to draw a clear separation of the Derridean and Lacanian problematics that are so entangled theoretically. Furthermore, although Derrida rejects the category of the Lacanian subject, it is not even that difference that cleanly marks the split between the two. In a 1988–1989 interview with Jean-Luc Nancy, published in *Who Comes after the Subject*, Derrida pushes against what he sees as Nancy's too quick philosophical dismissal of the subject, noting the difference between the metaphysical subject and the idea of the subject that has emerged in various ways from Heidegger's existential analytic:

> I am thinking of those today who would try to reconstruct a discourse around a subject that would not be predeconstructive, around a subject that would no longer include the figure of mastery of self, of adequation to self . . . but which would define the subject rather as the finite experience of nonidentity to self, as the underivable interpellation inasmuch as it comes from the other, from the trace of the other, with all the paradoxes or the aporia of being-before-the-law.[89]

Given the Lacanian resonances in this comment, one might wonder how radical the break between Derrida and Lacan actually is. Unless, of course, one returns to "Le Facteur de la vérité," where one encounters the radical rupture having to do with the phallus, and with two incommensurate readings of sexual difference. Indeed, as a question of *reading*, the break Johnson points to recalls the break that Marx locates in his reading of the classical political economists, who stumble at the two incommensurable problematics of capitalist and pre-capitalist cost of labor, their question moving from one problematic to another without registering the move. Citing again Marx's reading: "The question unconsciously substituted itself in Political Economy for the original one: for the search after the cost of production of labour as such turned in a circle and never left the spot."[90]

While the Derridean and Lacanian problematics are clearly not separated by the same historical shift, the stumble that Johnson points to in Derrida's reading of Lacan — the stumble that marks the impasse — is formally similar. In "The Frame of Reference," Johnson stages the break between Derrida and Lacan at the nexus of reading, sexual difference, and meaning — a break that turns on the reading of two sentences of Lacan's. The first, from "The Signification of the Phallus," is the sentence on the basis of which Derrida indicts Lacan of "phallogocentristic transcendentalism": "The phallus is the privileged signifier of that mark where logos is joined together with the advent of desire."[91] For Derrida once again, the sentence provides evidence that given the psychoanalytic context, "the privileged locus for this privileged signifier is the voice,"[92] the transmitter of desire; and that through the voice the phonemic structure of language does its phallic work of supporting the "drive of the proper" that underpins the subject. Seen this way, only dissemination can "mutilate" the unity of the phallus.

In a move not unlike that of Marx's reading, Johnson challenges Derrida's straightforward reading by signaling a dislocation within the sentence in question:

> The important word in this definition is *joined*. For if language (alienation of needs through the place of the Other) and desire (the remainder that is left after

the subtraction of real needs from absolute demand) are neither totally separable from each other nor related in the same way to their own division, the phallus is the signifier of the articulation between two very problematic chains.[93]

After juxtaposing her reading of Lacan's sentence to Derrida's, in which the phallus as "privileged signifier" is in the service of metaphysical closure, Johnson goes on to ask just what is a *signifier*? Not surprisingly, Lacan's defining sentence — "A signifier is what represents a subject for another signifier" — offers an even more dramatic example of syntactical dislocation.[94] Johnson observes how difficult it is to register the relationships between "subject" and "signifier" in this sentence since the two terms are neither fully separated nor entirely fused, that is, the distinction between "subject" and "signifier" in the first part of the sentence is subverted in the second part.

"There are three positions in the definition," Johnson writes,

two of which are occupied by the same word, but the word is differentiated from itself in the course of the definition — because it begins to take the place of the *other* word. The signifier for which the other signifier represents a subject thus acts like a subject because it is the place where the representation is "understood." The signifier, then, situates the place of something like a reader. And the reader becomes the place where representation would be understood if there were any such thing as a place beyond representation. . . ."[95]

In Johnson's reading, the purloined letter-as-signifier-as-phallus is "thus not a thing or the absence of a thing, not a word or the absence of a word, not an organ or the absence of an organ, but a *knot* in a structure where words, things, and organs can neither be definitely separated nor completely contained."[96] The letter-signifier is hidden, but not in the normal spatial sense of the word; it is hidden in a symbolic structure, "a structure that can only be perceived in its effects, and whose effects are perceived as repetition." Psychoanalysis, she goes on, "is the repetition of a *trauma of interpretation* — called 'castration', or 'parental coitus' or 'the Oedipus complex' or even 'sexuality'— the traumatic deferred interpretation not *of* an event, but as an event that never took place as such." Such an event she calls "an interpretive infelicity whose result was to situate the interpreter in an intolerable position."[97]

If Derrida's position as a reader of Lacan seems quite tolerable, it is because, as Johnson says, he takes the letter-signifier-phallus not as an articulation of two problematic chains, but as a *substance*, which is why he argues so with Lacan's insistence that the letter is both material and that it cannot be divided. But for Lacan, it is the not the letter's substance that matters, and not its contents, but rather the rhetorical position in which it puts each of its holders. Johnson writes:

> Therefore, by saying that the letter cannot be divided Lacan does not mean that the phallus must remain intact, but that the phallus and the letter and the signifier *are not substances*. The letter cannot be divided because it only functions as a division. It is not something with "an *identity* to itself inaccessible to dismemberment" (. . . emphasis mine) as Derrida interprets it; it is a *difference*. It is known only in its effects. The signifier is an articulation in a chain, not an identifiable unit.[98]

Once again, Derrida's reading of Lacan gives pause. How can the Derrida of invagination, of the hymen, find substances in the texts in question rather than the effects of difference? How can the author of *Spurs: Nietzsche's Styles* hypostasize this reading of sexual difference? In *Spurs*, first given as a lecture ("La Question du style") in 1972, three years before the first publication of "Le Facteur de la vérité," Derrida explores Nietzsche's multiple and contradictory writings on woman in a richly mobile and seductive text that undermines any suggestion of the positivity of sexual difference. At the very time Lacan declares in *Encore* (1972–73) "[t]here is no such thing as Woman,"[99] Derrida writes that if one must keep one's distance from the "feminine operation," "it is perhaps because 'woman' is not some thing, the determinable identity of a figure that appears in the distance."[100]

Of course, such thematic similarities between Derrida's woman and Lacan's woman only serve to cover over the interpretive impasse Johnson points to. Derrida's reading of Nietzsche's warring invocations of woman produces a text in which *la* femme does not exist because for this woman there is no truth in castration. For her "castration *does not take place, has no place*," a formula, Derrida writes, that "marks first of all that the place of castration is not determinable: an undecidable mark or non-mark. . . ." Derrida goes on, "Nietzsche did not delude himself into thinking he knew what was going on with the effects called woman, truth, castration, or the *ontological* effects of presence or absence."[101] In short, the woman in *Spurs* figures the undoing of phallogocentrism:

> From the moment the question of woman suspends the decidable opposition of the true and the non-true, from the moment it installs the epochal regime of quotation marks for all the concepts belonging

to this system of philosophical decidability, once it
disqualifies the hermeneutic project that postulates
a true meaning of a text and liberates reading from
the horizon of the meaning of being or the truth of
being . . . from that moment what is unleashed is the
question of style as a question of writing, the question of a spurring operation more powerful than any
context, any thesis, or any meaning.[102]

If Lacan's woman bears the truth of what Johnson calls
the impossible "trauma of interpretation" ("called 'castration' . . . or even 'sexuality'"), Derrida's undoes philosophical decidability, suspending the decidable opposition of
truth and non-truth. Here at last, then, is the difference between the Derridean and the Lacanian readings of sexual
difference: the difference between two versions of the impossible: the *undecidable* and what Lacan calls the *Real*.

In the split between sexual difference as undecidable and
sexual difference as Real lies the impasse between deconstruction and psychoanalysis, the impasse that can once
again be obscured by Derrida's complicated relationship
to psychoanalysis. It can be baffling, indeed, to follow Derrida's conflicting positions, as Geoffrey Bennington demonstrates in his canny reading of the question. In a chapter
titled "Circanalysis (the thing itself)," Bennington patiently
traces Derrida's seeming inconsistencies. In spite of Derrida's huge debt to Freud, Bennington writes, "there is, and
would have been, no Derrida without Freud."[103] In spite of
Derrida's acknowledgment that Freud fundamentally puts
into question "the primacy of presence as consciousness,"
Bennington writes, citing Derrida's words from *Différance*,[104]
he never retreats from his judgment that Freudian concepts
all belong, in Derrida's words, "without exception, to the

history of metaphysics, that is, to the system of logocentric repression. . . ."[105]

This is not in itself surprising in that Derrida acknowledges that one never leaves metaphysics, that even a neologism like *différance* "remains a metaphysical name."[106] What matters is Derrida's accompanying judgment. Repeatedly he lauds a Freudian concept, such as *Nachtraglichkeit*, only to remark that it is a "conceptual schema unequal to the thing itself."[107] His objection is commonly that psychoanalysis does not reflect adequately on its relationship to metaphysics, that it achieves insights critical of metaphysics only to back off, failing to reflect on "the thing itself."

Given that objection, what do we make, Bennington asks, of Freud's comment in *Beyond the Pleasure Principle* that he regrets his need to use the figurative language of depth psychology, which cannot fail to oversimplify his speculations? It would be different, Freud writes, if the language of physics or chemistry — figurative but less problematic — were already available to him. Even better if biological science were to open up its many possibilities. But given his limitations, he can only labor in a discourse that inevitably reduces his speculations to the banality of the known.[108]

Derrida's reaction in "To Speculate — on 'Freud'" is to label those comments of Freud's as no more than "a very classical logic," in which provisional suspense simply leads to proper containment through "metaphoric transfer."[109] But is there not another way of reading Freud's remarks, Bennington asks, a way supported by the note that ends the chapter in question, about which Derrida says little? In that note Freud underlines the problem of metaphoricity by putting "life instinct" and "death instinct" in quotation marks, and then goes on to write: "These speculations seek to solve the riddle of life by supposing that these two instincts were struggling with each other from the very first."[110] As Bennington comments, "It would be just this inequality or originary non-originarity that would constitute Freud's call, of which we could now say that the fact of its being unequal to the thing itself constitutes, precisely, its originality."[111]

Following this, Bennington immediately writes that he is not doing what some other of Derrida's readers do — from de Man to Johnson to Žižek — namely accuse Derrida of finding metaphysical blindness where it doesn't exist. Of course, Bennington is doing just that, but with the difference that in this case he sees in Derrida's readings the trace of a "singular, original, nervous relation between psychoanalysis and deconstruction": "This resistance . . . would become something like a principle of undecidability or interminability, both what undoes the very principle of analysis and affirms it in its very interminability, a so to speak internal resistance of psychoanalysis to psychoanalysis, the relaunched singularity that relaunches the theory as a call always, structurally, unequal to the thing itself."[112]

Bennington goes on to say that had Derrida not resisted Freud, had he not turned around him interminably, "he would not have been able to think the structures of resistance to the call of metaphysics which define deconstruction in general. . . ."[113] This reading of Bennington's is not unlike Johnson's observation that in accusing psychoanalysis of always finding itself, Derrida actually expresses a profound insight into the essence of psychoanalysis — as the repetition of a "traumatic deferred interpretation not *of* an event, but *as* an event that never took place as such."[114]

One might argue that Derrida's interminable undecidable amounts to something like the psychoanalytic impossible. There is a difference, however, that has to do with their differing relationships to metaphysics. As Roudinesco so astutely points out, in Freud's inability to bring psychoanalysis into the natural sciences, he invented metapsychology at the intersection of science and speculative reflection: "Hence the idea of translating metaphysics into a metapsychology, that is, of renouncing the knowledge of being for that of unconscious processes."[115] Thus, while Derrida *challenges* the knowledge of being, the psychoanalytic turn to the unconscious entails a *renunciation* of that knowledge. It is, indeed, the difference between these two moves that renders the reading practices of Derrida and Lacan incommensurable. One engages with the undecidability that dooms any effort to express a self-present truth (of being) within the differential structure of language, the other deals with an impossibility internal to the unconscious.

First, the Derridean undecidable. Derrida was certainly not alone in displacing the subject onto something like a "scriptural subjectivity." Jacqueline Rose cites the following passage from Paul de Man to illustrate how strong the move was at the time to absorb psychoanalysis into deconstruction: "Far from seeing language as an instrument in the service of a psychic energy," de Man writes, "the possibility now arises that the entire construction of the drive, substitutions, repressions, and representations is the aberrant, metaphorical correlative of the absolute randomness of language, prior to any figuration or meaning."[116] De Man makes the comment in a reading of Rousseau's *Confessions* in which he shows how the metaphorical dimension of the text is displaced by the more "machinal" structural elements: "The deconstruction of the figural dimension is a process that takes place independently of any desire; as such, it is not unconscious but mechanical, systematic in its performance but arbitrary in its principle, like a grammar. This threatens the autobiographical subject not as the loss of something that was once present and that it once possessed, but as a radical estrangement between the meaning and the performance of any text."[117]

If for de Man, then, psychoanalytic theories of the subject are the metaphoric correlative of the randomness of language, that is to say of structural elements of language that do their work prior to figuration or meaning, the psychoanalytic subject is thus doubly secondary to language, and as the structural correlative of language, the operations of which are prior to figuration of meaning, its presumption of unconscious motivation is "aberrant."

Derrida figures the work of language a bit differently. For him, as we have seen, language is the site of a life and death struggle, where the originary structural working of "survival" is there to be confronted. For him, a generalized writing stages the *différance* that Western philosophy is so resistant to in its investment in meaning without difference from itself. Writing stages "the play of a trace," Derrida writes, "which no longer belongs to the horizon of Being, but whose play transports and encloses the meaning of Being: the play of the trace, or the *différance*, which has no meaning and is not. Which does not belong. There is no maintaining, and no depth to, this bottomless chessboard on which Being is put into play."[118]

Borrowing liberally from Freud, Derrida conceives of *différance* as a *scriptural unconscious*. He conceives it in line with Freud's structure of delay (*Nachträglichkeit*): as a radical alternative to presence and absence, an alterity "with a 'past' that has never been present." He takes from Freud an unconscious "that differs from and defers itself," sending out "delegates, representatives, proxies; but without any chance that the giver of proxies might 'exist' might be present . . . and with even less chance that it might become conscious." This is where Derrida maintains that he improves on Freud in his conviction that however carefully theorized the psychic subject might be, it cannot escape the pitfalls of the phenomenal: for "[i]n order to read the traces of 'unconscious traces' (there are no 'conscious' traces), the language of presence and absence, the metaphysical discourse of phenomenology is inadequate."[119]

"Undecidable" is the term Derrida gives to textual indeterminacy, not as a sign of some "inexhaustible ambivalence" of a word,[120] but in the structural sense of something like a double bind, the textual double bind in which the reader is inscribed. Kamuf compares the performance of the Derridean reader to the act of looking for the dictionary definition of "reader": "before one can receive the order of the concept, one has already given an example of it."[121]

Derrida explores this full-blown indeterminacy in "The Double Session." There he brings together Mallarmé's *Mimique* and an excerpt from Plato's *Philebus* that evokes various mimetic hierarchies. Unsurprisingly, philosophical determinacy is undone by poetic enactments of undecidability. Derrida manages, as Johnson writes in her introduction to *Dissemination*, to both preserve and erase the difference between imitation and imitated so that the mime's operation is seen as "'a perpetual allusion' to himself on the point of alluding."[122] And as we saw earlier, the principal figure of undecidability that Derrida reads in Mallarmé's text is that of the hymen, which marks the *entre*, the *between* that both joins and separates like other doubly contradictory words in Derrida's critical lexicon: pharmakon, supplement, and, of course, *différance*. But again, as Derrida stresses, what unsettles the text is not simply semantic ambivalence but undecidable syntax, "an irreducible excess of the syntactic over the semantic": "The word 'between' has no full meaning of its own. *Inter* acting forms a syntactical plug; not a categorem, but a syncategorem." Hymen, like the other "double-edged" words are both contradictory and non-contradictory: "Without any dialectical *Aufhebung*, without any time off, they belong in a sense both to consciousness and to the unconscious, which Freud tells us can tolerate or remain insensitive to contradiction. Insofar as the text depends upon them, bends to them [s'y plié], it thus plays a double scene upon a double stage."[123]

To move from Derrida's undecidability to the Lacanian Real is to enter a different problematic. Roudinesco makes it clear that in renouncing "the knowledge of being" for that of the unconscious, Freud dissociated psychoanalysis from both psychology and philosophy, inventing metapsychology at the intersection of the natural sciences and speculative reflection. The specificity of that intersection is crucial. In the words of Laplanche and Pontalis, "[m]etapsychology constructs an ensemble of conceptual models which are more or less far-removed from empirical reality," including the "fiction of a psychical apparatus," and so forth. Laplanche and Pontalis go on to observe that the way "metapsychology" echoes "metaphysics" was not unintentional, that Freud indeed undertook to "redress the constructions of metaphysics," which he viewed as unconscious projections, and that his pursuit of the unconscious was an effort to get beyond the limits of the perception-consciousness system.[124]

Of course, Freud dismantles the mind-body split—the essence of the metaphysical—from the outset, as Laplanche underlines in *Life and Death in Psychoanalysis*. There Laplanche shows how the Freudian drive is "propped up" on a vital bodily function, "how emergent sexuality attaches itself to and is propped up upon another process which is both similar and profoundly divergent."[125] It is thus that Laplanche contrasts the fantasmatic breast—the object of the oral sexual drive—with the natural breast, noting "that on the one hand there is from the beginning an object, but that on the other hand sexuality does not have, from the beginning, a real object."[126] To recall Zupančič's words, sexuality is out-of-joint not because of some metaphysical mind-body split, but on the contrary, because the vital and the psychical "originate from the same place."[127]

Zupančič goes on to offer a reading of how Lacan theorizes this early out-of-jointness of sexuality through his eventual formulation of the Real, which he aligns with the "impossible."[128] By reframing Freud's theorization of sexuality in terms of the Real, Lacan aims to rescue it from humanistic and psychologistic reduction and to restore its radicality. Recognizing that Lacan's own formulation can be susceptible to commonsense (metaphysical) understandings of the Real as "outside" or "beyond" symbolization, Zupančič focuses on Lacan's attention to the gap constitutive of signification (another way of expressing the constitutive lack in the Other).[129] She writes that "the signifying order is coextensive with a gap," that it begins with a "minus-one," that it has "the lack of a signifier 'built into it,' so to speak,"[130] marking the discursive structure in significant ways:

> It marks (and thus effectively "curves") it by sticking to a certain set (or chain) of other signifiers that relate in some way to this lack of a signifier. The way enjoyment relates to (or is linked to) the signifying order passes through what is missing in this order; it does not relate to it directly but via its constitutive negativity (a minus one). This negativity is the Real of the junction between the (missing) signifier and enjoyment; and the conceptual name for this configuration in psychoanalysis is sexuality (or the sexual).[131]

Zupančič is very clear that sexuality is *not* missing a signifier. It is not something that the signifying order might represent but fails to do so, and that is because "the sexual is not some extradiscursive object lacking a signifier; rather, it is a direct *consequence* ('extension') of the missing of a signifier; that is, of the gap with which the signifying order emerges.... To spell it out in full: human sexuality is the placeholder of the missing signifier." Sexuality is messy, she goes on, but that messiness is "the sewing up of the gap."[132]

The Real is where the missing signifier meets enjoyment, or where, as Zupančič says, "surplus-enjoyment ... emerges at the place of the signifying deficit or hole."[133]

And if the Lacanian (split) subject emerges with the minus-one of signification, Lacanian castration, Zupančič writes, "is a subjectivising reiteration of the inaugurating minus."[134] To grasp how this works, how sexual difference is inextricable from the constitutive "lack" that is built into discourse, we recall that Lacan formulates the phallus as the signifier of splitting, of the wedding of logos to the advent of desire. To recall Rose's words, "the phallus relegates sexuality to a strictly other dimension — the order of the symbolic outside of which, for Lacan, sexuality cannot be understood. The importance of the phallus is that its status in the development of human sexuality is something which nature *cannot* account for."[135]

What is so striking about this formulation — what renders it "impossible" in the most intriguing way is that while nature cannot account for the phallus that signifies the division of castration, neither can the very symbolic order to which it is relegated. That is to say, subjects "make sense" of sexuality in the symbolic but the symbolic makes no sense of sexuality. As Rose writes, Lacan takes language in two directions: "towards the fixing of meaning itself (that which is enjoined on the subject), and away from that very fixing to the point of its constant slippage, the risk or vanishing point which it always contains (the unconscious). Sexuality is placed on both these dimensions at once."[136]

It is in the play of these two dimensions that Lacan locates the impossible Real of sexual difference. And it is as an effect of discourse, in relation to the phallus, that the subject's masculine or feminine position is inscribed as castration. Any male privilege derived from the phallus is, in Rose's word, a sham. As to the feminine: "As the place onto which loss is projected, and through which it is simultaneously disavowed, woman is a 'symptom' for the man."[137] In other words, "woman" occupies the place of the *objet a*, "Lacan's formula for the lost object which underpins symbolization, cause of and 'stand-in' for desire."[138]

Frida Saal's paper on Lacan and Derrida closes with the suggestion that "the main difference that remains in the field cultivated by Lacan and Derrida, is Lacan's elaboration of the objet a, a necessary loss for the existence of the subject."[139] The *objet a* does, indeed, mark the divergence between two different reading strategies. As we have seen, the deconstructive reading displaces the subject of the unconscious along with the phenomenological subject. This allows de Man to assert that the psychical subject is merely the correlative of the workings of language, and a misleading one at that, given that language's deconstruction of the figural dimension is independent of any desire, "not unconscious but mechanical, systematic in its performance but arbitrary in its principle, like a grammar."[140]

Derrida's reading of the Freudian unconscious leads him to modify de Man's rigor somewhat, enlivening the mechanical with the play of *différance*. For Derrida, the scene of *écriture* is dynamic and ultimately lethal, a "bottomless chessboard on which Being is put into play," never to be joined to meaning.[141] His is not the impassive de Manean reader who never fails to render the affective mechanical. Derrida's reader sees the play of *différance* as a life and death drama that he reads as a *witness*. Agency is involved but as an imperative: it is the Necessity that Derrida invokes in his description of what drives him. Without deconstructive vigilance, language might lead him to forget that his own desire for good, his own metaphysics of presence "not only cannot be accomplished, meets its limit, but should not be accomplished — because the accomplishment or the fulfillment of this desire for presence would be Death itself."[142] So whether we are looking at de Man's refusal of affect or Derrida's engagement with it, deconstruction entails the same linguistic structure that inexorably undoes figurative workings of meaning. Only the most attentive, the most rigorous can guard against the pitfalls of naïve reading, of naïve knowing.

With Lacan, attentiveness and rigor have little to offer. For the Lacanian subject — that is to say, the subject of the unconscious — the stakes of knowing are impossible and impossibly immanent.[143] Produced by the symbolic, an effect of language, the psychoanalytic subject can be said to inhabit the Real, that gap built into the symbolic order. To inhabit the gap is to inhabit the treachery of signification; it is not to know what one knows or to know what one does not know one knows. Consider again Lacan's formulation that "a signifier is what represents a subject for another signifier" and Johnson's comments on the syntactical dislocation involved therein: "The signifier for which the other signifier represents a subject acts like a subject because it is the place where the representation is 'understood.' The signifier, then, situates the place of something like a reader. And the reader becomes the place where representation would be understood if there were any such thing as a place beyond representation. . . ."[144]

The reader is caught then in an impossibility that Johnson calls the "trauma of interpretation," the repetition of which could be called "castration" or even "sexuality." It is sexual division as castration that dislocates interpretation and makes it so impossible, so impervious to efforts to close the split with any kind of yin-and-yang complementarity. If for Derrida the masculine/feminine binary is a phallogocentric fraud, for Lacan it speaks through the Real. In Zupančič's words: the signifying order emerges "with the lack of a signifier 'built into it,' so to speak (a signifier which, if it existed, would be the 'binary signifier')."[145] This is what Lacan aims to figure in his sexuation formula, a formula that shows, as Zupančič says, "how the constitutive minus of the signifying order is inscribed in this order itself, and dealt with." If the Woman is the Other of Man, the reverse is not the case. There is no second sex, Zupančič writes: "What splits into two is the very nonexistence of the one (that is, of the one which, if it existed would be the Other, the radically Other)."[146]

3
Reading the Stamp of History

What the debate between Derrida and Lacan reveals is an impasse on either side of the differences/difference deadlock. Unencumbered by the political complexities of the feminist debates, the deconstructive and psychoanalytic readings move relentlessly to their own impasses in the undecidable and the Real respectively. In doing so, they expose the way the disruptive power of sexual difference can work in two different registers of signification. At the same time, the Derridean and Lacanian readings put into relief the dynamic relationships between interpretive impossibility and critical reading, the complex possibilities of impossibility, as it were. It is this reanimation of interpretive impossibility that is crucial not only for the future of feminist politics, but for the future of reading.

A call for reading the impossible—for more critique in other words—need not be a simple dismissal of current calls for something different. Critique and post-critique are connected. Both renewed turns to critique and turns away from it are efforts to grapple with interpretive impasses. And in their grappling, both bear in different ways the historical stamp of advanced capitalism in its neoliberal form of legibility. And both bear the stamp of the modern episteme in which it is not transparent truth that we find but *knowledge effects* produced by structures of signification. It is thus that for Lacan knowledge is an effect of the structure of the unconscious, for Derrida an effect of the traces of signification. And it is thus that the complex, overdetermined knowledge effects that make up the current capitalist conjuncture are so fully implicated in debates about critical reading. For these reasons I will look at some of the ways critique and post-critique bear the stamp of history, asking both how they *bear* the stamp and how they *read* it. To this end, I bring together, on the one hand, the modes of critique that animate feminist impossibility—deconstruction and psychoanalysis—and, on the other, surface reading and the new materialisms.

I begin with an essay by Walter Benn Michaels that is engaged with the interpretive trickiness of reading the stamp of history. The essay, "Meaning and Affect," was written to accompany a 2019 show at LAXART by the artist Phil Chang. Titled *Cache, Active*, the show is a series of photographs and photograms that expose and fade in the light, leaving reddish brown monochromes. What interests Michaels is the complex play in these pieces between the performance of fading and the final object, a play that involves paradoxical relationships of immateriality and materiality. One way of describing *Cache, Active*, Michaels writes, would be to align it with artistic imperatives to resist representation, that is to say—citing Tom McCarthy citing Simon Critchley—to let "matter matter."[1] Such a critical view, he notes, would be in line with Best and Marcus's essay "Surface Reading," with its debts to Susan Sontag's 1966 *Against Interpretation*.[2] Looking at Chang's work this way, the fading photographs "don't just let matter matter, they make metaphor, meaning and representation itself into matter," that is, what the work is about — the difference between what it is and what it represents — disappears leaving behind a material remnant in the form of the monochromes.

Yet, this older reading against representation, however persuasive, doesn't work, Michaels writes, because the remaining monochromes mark to varying degrees the effacement of the original images. The final monochromes "are, in a certain sense, abstractions, in a kind of variation on the old Lacanian formula — 'the symbol manifests itself first of all as the murder of the thing.'"[3] Thus, "what we get here is a thing that (in order to mean) cannot simply be, i.e. a thing determined in its being as much by what it isn't as by what it is." For Michaels then, Chang's encounter with meaning is very different from that of the early postmodernists — a difference, one might say, that has to do with the stamp of history. Referring to Douglas Crimp's 1996 *On the Museum's Ruins*, Michaels writes:

> It was once possible for a writer like Douglas Crimp to imagine a truly "materialist critique of art" (his exemplary instance was Serra) that would resist the "idealism of modern sculpture" (Caro) and seek "to defeat consumption altogether" — that would replace the experience of art as a "luxury commodity" with "the experience of art in its material reality." Today that ship has sailed to, and then back from, Shenzhen.[4]

The difference between Chang and earlier artists, Michaels argues, is that Chang, born in 1974, has never known an art world that did not insist on the literal in one way or another. But the difference between Chang's art world and the earlier era is a change in "meaningfulness" — a change not just art historical but economic. However you measure the growth of capitalism, Michaels writes — whether through extreme inequality in the US or through its global purchase — the penetration of the market in every form of production, including the production of art, "is complete in a way that seemed almost unimaginable in the late 60s and early 70s."

With the commodity, Michaels reminds us, all that matters is that it is sold, which means that postmodern concerns such as a critique of artistic intentionality turn out to be fully consistent with commodity logic. In an era of full market penetration, the only resistance to the artistic commodity, the only thing that is not reducible to commodity logic is its *meaning* — and what *Cache, Active* offers is an encounter with meaning:

> This is what is at stake in the encounter [Chang's pictures] stage with their own materiality; the felt power of the reduction of being is what gives their insistence on meaning its force. And it's also why the sense of loss as the original image fades is crucial but not dispositive: we can't help feeling something but it doesn't matter what we feel. And like the disarticulation of meaning from being, the disarticulation of meaning from feeling requires an encounter with its appeal. It's only the intimacy with what it doesn't do that makes it possible for *Cache, Active* to do what it does.

It is not that Chang's work claims some fantasmatic outside to commodity logic, but rather that it provides an angle from which to confront it, an angle that in Michaels's reading exposes the dated nature of the earlier postmodern turn to the material. Indeed, with the saturation of capital, the postmodern aesthetic can seem redundant in its reflection of commodity logic.

Michaels's move from reading *Cache, Active* as congruent with the postmodern artistic and critical embrace of the literal, to an understanding of Chang's work as something quite different, is a move fully driven by the stamp of history, which for Michaels, is marked by the precipitous growth of economic inequality in the US and the global dominance of capitalism. Hence, the earlier call to let matter matter, to let it speak for itself, no long works, Michaels argues. Today it is the turn toward *meaning* that resists commodification, that opposes the commodity in which there is no meaning other than exchange value.[5]

The double reading that Michaels offers of *Cache, Active* is an illustration of his abiding argument that the aesthetic and the theoretical must also be read as *political* — the political grasped in relation to the historical advance of capitalism. And for Michaels, to read politically is to resist the collapse of meaning onto perceived context, for the collapse of work and world means the loss of the very space that makes critical thought possible — the space that separates work from world. For him, that crucial separation resists the lures of realism or recognition or identification, and opens up the possibility of analysis that could not be grasped otherwise. The separation opened up, he argues, is the intentional space of form, which is *about* something, and its "*aboutness* is what separates it from the thing it's of."[6]

Rather than aiming to display dreadful abuses, Michaels argues, what political art needs is something different: "Maybe what's needed is an art that's less interested in the abuses of the system than in the system itself, and maybe it's the effort to produce something utterly self-contained that enables us to see in art not just a reflection of our current form of neoliberal capitalism but also what Nick Brown has described as 'neoliberalism's other.'"[7]

Animated always by dialectical provocation, Michaels

exposes the ways a collapse between text and world, like art and world, produces the very opposite of its critical intent.[8] When the text becomes a "thing," it becomes something that is "experienced" rather than understood, paradoxically reinforcing the very role of the subject that postmodernism had aimed to dethrone. He argues that the substitution of subject position (identity) for ideology (what we believe) results in the virtual neglect of the category of *class* — that is, the structure of capitalist exploitation — and substitutes competing experiences for competing analyses.[9]

Post-critique

If, as Michaels argues, the most recent stamp of history bears the full penetration of capital and its logic, what to make of "Surface Reading," which, in calling for the reader to focus on "what is evident, perceptible, apprehensible in texts," "what is neither hidden nor hiding," seems to engage in what Michaels calls a collapse of text and world. Unlike the art historical call to "let matter matter," however, which was a *challenge* to the logic of capital, "Surface Reading" seems to accept capital's success. Why look to expose hidden ideological structures, it asks, when social and political ills are there to be seen? Why be suspicious of false consciousness when all we need to do is read what is there? While deconstruction and psychoanalysis were critically useful in the past, it maintains, they have outlived their ability to reveal anything that is not before our eyes. Rather than pursue a "hermeneutics of suspicion," better to recognize the limits of criticism in the name of "political realism."[10]

But what if deconstructive and psychoanalytic readings turn out to be surface reading after all? And what if reading the surface tells us more about the "structure of capitalist exploitation" than "political realism" does?

To see surface reading as converging with deconstruction and psychoanalysis rather than a turning away, one must trouble the very question of surface and depth that frames the argument. One can do that quite efficiently by pointing out that the "symptomatic reading" on which the surface and depth frame revolves bears no resemblance to the mode of reading proposed by Althusser, who coined the term. For Althusser, symptomatic reading, or the reading of effects, is the only way to grasp the structure of a given problematic, that is, its problems and concepts as well as their absence. It is modeled, of course, on Freud's reading of what the patient's words reveal about the structure and workings of the unconscious.

Of even greater interest is the way the figure of surface and depth plays out in the post-critical call to leave depth behind. Citing Fredric Jameson's comment that interpretation should seek a "latent meaning behind a manifest one," the essay (mis)characterizes "symptomatic reading" as conflating three pairs of opposition: present/absent, manifest/latent, surface/depth. Although these oppositions are indeed distinct, as the essay points out; and although they point to different theories of reading, it is the essay, not "symptomatic reading" that conflates the three in its thematic framing.

What the essay also conflates is the difference between *theories* of reading and *modes* of reading. While deconstruction and psychoanalysis have different theories of reading—both of which differ from the theory of surface reading—all three can be said to share the same mode of surface reading. That is to say, neither the deconstructive nor the psychoanalytic mode of reading looks to a latent truth revealed by interpretation. To read that way would be, as Althusser says, to embrace the religious myth of reading in which the Logos speaks the Truth of Being.[11] It would be a pre-critical hermeneutic practice dedicated to obviating the "disarticulation of meaning and being," to borrow Michaels's words.

It is not surprising that psychoanalysis can be viewed as a depth hermeneutic given the numerous depth metaphors Freud employs to figure psychoanalytic concepts. One has only to think of analysis as an archeological dig or the mind as an iceberg with only one-seventh above water. But with the job of grasping the workings of the mind, it is surface reading, rather, that the analyst deploys in search of the truth of the unconscious. Recall Freud's insistence that to seek the essence of a dream one looks not to a latent content but to the "form of thinking" that is the dream, or what he calls the dream work that produces that form. And recall Lacan's insistence that to read the unconscious one looks not to what a sign points to ("where there's smoke there's fire"), but to the way the subject slides in the network of signifiers.

In the case of deconstructive surface reading, recall Derrida's reading of Mallarmé in which undecidability emerges from the "irreducible excess of the syntactic over the semantic." And recall the play of the trace of *différance*, "which has no meaning and is not. . . . There is no maintaining, and no depth to, this bottomless chessboard on which Being is put into play."[12]

Of course the most striking illustration of surface reading is Marx's. Recall the opening chapter of *Capital* that traces the soulless working of the commodity, the value of which is derived not from the useful depths of its being (as in the wooly warmth of the coat, for example), but from its exchange on the market. It is thus that Marx's surface reading of the commodity form exposes the structure of capitalist exploitation, or the logic by which profit is derived from the surplus value the laborer produces over wages received.

When Michaels suggests that Phil Chang's *Cache, Active* might be more effective political art than a display of capitalist abuses, it is not because *Cache, Active* contains some hidden meaning. It is because it stages a meaning there to be read, a meaning that bears the imprint of history. What is crucial, of course, is how *history* is understood. In a somewhat earlier critical time, the meaning of Marx's stamp of history was itself understood through the metaphor of depth, that is, through the figure of an economic base determining a cultural and political superstructure.[13] Once again, as with Freud's depth metaphors, it is not surprising that Marx's formulation of base and superstructure would invite such a reading, along with the notion of ideological false consciousness underpinning a hermeneutics of suspicion. But as with Freud, while the depth metaphor serves to figure a conceptual formulation, it does not dictate how its effects are to be read. And just as Marx could read his own break with the classical political economists, so was he able to put into question the workings of economic determinism. In Marx's analysis there is no clear, predictable separation of elements into the determining and the determined. To cite from the "Glossary" of *Reading Capital*, "The Marxist totality . . . is never separable in this way from the elements that constitute it, as each is the condition of existence of all the others."[14] Moreover, given that for Marx the relations of production always already entail the production of *knowledge*, the object of knowledge does not reside in the depths of time, waiting to be revealed anew to succeeding generations, but is produced — and read — with history.[15]

Viewed thusly, the very frame of surface and depth that underpins the call for surface reading can be seen as having been rendered outmoded by the stamp of history. But one need not look so far afield to notice trouble in the text of "Surface Reading." While, as Michaels observes, the essay bears some similarity to the historical call to "let matter matter," there are once again differences between the two. "Surface Reading's" call to 'let texts say what they say,' is not a challenge to commodification like the art historical stance; but neither does it abandon all search for meaning. Indeed, however modest its relationship to meaning compared to the earlier criticism it considers overreaching, it objects to being simply labeled as politically passive: "Surface reading, which strives to describe texts accurately, might easily be dismissed as politically quietist, too willing to accept things as they are. We want to reclaim from this tradition the accent on immersion in texts (without paranoia or suspicion about their merit or value), for we understand that attentiveness to the artwork as itself a kind of freedom."[16]

Considering this search for a kind of freedom, it could be argued that the framing conundrum of the essay is not so much 'how we read now' but 'why we read now.' If this is the case, the displacement of the essay's primary question (why we read) onto the frame of surface and depth (how we read), could be seen as turning a political question into a formal one—but one in which any actual *question* has been always already displaced onto the highly thematized notion of surface and depth. We might then see these displacements as forming a kind of warped frame, which, among other things, distorts the relationship between past and present critical readings, thus helping to explain how an otherwise critically astute essay can turn on a number of "misreadings."

Of course there are various types of "misreading." As distinct from a new or different meaning that is opened up by every reading—one never reads the same thing twice—a misreading misrepresents the working of a text so as to render it unrecognizable to itself. Among various types of misreading, there is the inadvertent; there is the deliberate; there is misreading that seems produced by a short circuit, as in Derrida's reading of Lacan on Poe; and there is misreading produced by a kind of defensive displacement, as in "Surface Reading."

While historical revisionism can involve all four of these types of misreading, the latter two are particularly curious. It is not surprising that Althusser, the dedicated reader of reading, offers some insights into this curiosity. In an essay on Marx and Freud, he suggests that in certain conflictual theories — one could include deconstruction along with Marxism and psychoanalysis — "attempts at annexation and revision are more interesting than simple attacks and criticisms."[17] Focusing on Freudian theory, which from the beginning "has provoked not only strong resistance, not only attacks and criticisms but, what is more interesting, attempts at *annexation* and revision," Althusser writes:

"I say that the attempts at annexation and revision are more interesting than simple attacks and criticisms, for they signify that Freudian theory contains, by the admission of its adversaries, something *true* and dangerous. Where there is nothing true, there is no reason to annex or revise. There is therefore something true in Freud that must get appropriated but in order that its meaning may be revised, for this truth is dangerous; it must be revised in order to be neutralized."[18]

Read through the stamp of history, "Surface Reading" may well be more "interesting" than it claims. For far from being the site of liberation, in these times the surface, like the face of the commodity, is precisely where the danger lies.

The "new materialist" or "new realist" turns raise a different set of questions. If "surface reading" can be said to confront the epistemological split of meaning and being with a kind of pragmatic acceptance, the new materialisms challenge the very terms of the split. One example is *The Speculative Turn: Continental Materialism and Realism*, edited by Levi Bryant, Nick Srnicek, and Graham Harman. The editors ground their turn on an unambiguous break: "While it is difficult to find a single adequate name . . . we propose 'The

Speculative Turn' as a deliberate counterpart to the now tiresome 'Linguistic Turn.'" The blurb on the book's back cover continues the "tiresome" motif: "It might be hard to find many shared positions in the writings [of the contributors] but what is missing from their positions is an obsession with the critique of written texts."[19]

Of course more is at stake than impatience with critical practices that have become tiresome in their familiarity: "By contrast with the repetitive continental focus on texts, discourses, social practices, and human finitude, the new breed of thinkers is turning once more to reality itself."[20] By deft opposition, the statements make it clear that the problem with the obsessive critique of language is its concomitant relationship to human finitude; and the problem with both: the blockage of reality. While continental philosophy dismantled traditional idealism, the editors note, it fell into its own anti-realist practice of "correlationism," Quentin Meillassoux's idea "according to which we only ever have access to the correlate between thinking and being, and never to either term apart from the other."[21]

The editors hasten to explain that the turn to speculation does not hold out some pre-critical escape from finitude's limits. Their wager is, rather, that moving attention from the epistemological to the ontological may yield salutary returns. The stakes are seen as high, both in this volume and elsewhere, as in *Vibrant Matter*, where Jane Bennett warns against "human hubris and our earth-destroying fantasies of conquest and consumption."[22] Such concern is commonly framed by two narratives regarding the troublesome place of the human. The first narrative, paraphrased by Zupančič, is that "since Descartes we have lost the *great Outside*, the absolute outside, the Real, and have become prisoners of our own subjective or *discursive cage[,]*" a claustrophobic and potentially lethal cage.[23] The second narrative is the need, as

Levi Bryant writes in *The Democracy of Objects*, for "a finally subjectless object," and for an object-oriented ontology.[24]

Whatever urgency the two framing narratives express, however, it is not clear that they can escape their own limits. For while "object-oriented" discourses can shift the critical focus and can look to alternative modes of analysis (such as in some quarters cybernetics or assemblage theory), they cannot dislodge the "correlationist" impasse. Indeed, the aim to access the great Outside by putting the subject under erasure and generalizing the object in no way escapes the co-relational structure of subject-object, but simply reinforces it.

What makes Quentin Meillassoux's speculative realism so different is his effort to address the correlationist impasse from within. His *After Finitude: An Essay on the Necessity of Contingency* is more than a thematically driven challenge to correlationism; it is radically and flamboyantly anti-Kantian. The oxymorons, or condensed paradoxes, that govern the text (after finitude; the necessity of contingency) are there to be unraveled. With elegance and panache, Meillassoux aims for reversal, to produce radical change by moving backward. Which means that what presides over the text is a quip of Hegel's that he cites at the very beginning: "We cannot represent the 'in itself' without it becoming 'for us,' or as Hegel amusingly put it, we cannot 'creep up on' the object 'from behind' so as to find out what it is in itself."[25] And yet, creeping up from behind is just what Meillassoux sets out to do.

He begins the book with a section titled "Ancestrality," declaring that his aim is to revive the Cartesian object as a material body with inherent properties. He insists that it is in fact possible to grasp how thought is able to access an *absolute*, that is to say, a being "whose separateness from thought is such that it presents itself to us as non-relative to us, as . . . existing whether we exist or not."[26] It is necessary to grasp this, Meillassoux says, because if we can't think anything that is absolute, we can't make sense of what science tells us about ancestrality—any reality anterior to the appearance of the human species or any recognized form of life.[27]

So it is *science* that concerns Meillassoux, or, more accurately, the always vexed relationship between science and philosophy. To understand science for Meillassoux is to understand modern science, that is, science since Galileo and the mathematization of nature. Accordingly, when he speaks of grasping the in-itself, he refers to those aspects that are mathematically formulated, arguing that "all those aspects of the object that can be formulated in mathematical terms can be meaningfully conceived as properties of the object in itself." So while sensible or secondary qualities exist only as a relation to a subject, mathematizable properties are exempt from the constraint of such a relation.

Meillassoux's entire effort, he writes near the end of the essay, is to bring philosophy more in line with science and to undo what he calls the Kantian catastrophe, which goes something like this: the Copernico-Galilean event (as he calls it) exposes the vanity of every attempt to provide a metaphysical foundation for physics. The subsequent Hume-event ratifies the first event "by demonstrating the fallaciousness of all metaphysical forms of rationality, which is to say ... the fallaciousness of the absoluteness of sufficient reason,"[28] or the principle according to which for everything "there must be a reason why it is thus and so rather than otherwise"—with each reason requiring a reason and so on, leading ultimately to the ontological reason, which alone can provide a perfect sole cause that is the cause of itself.[29] This principle of sufficient reason is what the Hume event undoes, in Hume's claim that the "world's being thus and so can only be discovered by way of experience, it cannot be demonstrated to be absolutely necessary."[30]

Meillassoux complains that instead of the Kant-event bringing philosophy into line with science at that crucial moment, it turns correlational knowledge into the *only* philosophically legitimate form of knowledge, the only licit form of philosophy being the henceforth *conditional* knowledge of our relation-to-the-world. It makes the mistake of taking the end of speculative metaphysics to be the end of the absolute. But, as Meillassoux asserts, while all metaphysics are speculative (speculation being "the type of thinking that claims to be able to access some form of the absolute") not all speculation is metaphysical. The collapse of the principle of sufficient reason does not, for Meillassoux, equal thought's inability to access the absolute.[31]

As to ancestrality — reality anterior to human life — science and philosophy approach the question in very different ways, Meillassoux writes, the difference being that for the scientist, the ancestral designates the *absence of givenness as such*. Although ancestrality is a temporal notion, for science, its definition invokes not distance in time, but *anteriority* in time. In short, it is *not the time of consciousness, but the time of science* and this time of science allows for a break between the scientific statement and its referent. In the discourse of the physicist, Meillassoux says, the mathematical statement about matter is Cartesian, not Pythagorean, that is to say, the claim is not that the being of accretion is *inherently* mathematical — that the numbers or equations exist in themselves. The physicist's statements remain ideal, he says, insofar as their reality is one of signification. The claim is, rather, that the statements designate *actual properties of the referent*. Meillassoux grants that the scientific statements are revisable, of course, if falsified and supplanted, but the relationship between statement and referent *remains one of truth and not correlation*.

What is so interesting in Meillassoux's formulation is precisely the relationship between the physicist's (mathematical) statements and the real referent. As Zupančič notes in her discussion of *After Finitude*, while the relationship between the Absolute and mathematics is still something of a discursive correlation, it is not a relationship of co-dependence. Rather than looking for something *beyond* the discursive, she writes, Meillassoux looks to their joint articulation, "which would escape the logic of transcendental constitution and hence of their co-dependence."[32]

Given this, Zupančič finds it curious that Meillassoux does not give more attention to the way science actually works, arguing that Lacan's notion of the Real corresponds more fully to the actual practice of modern science. The difference between Lacan and Meillassoux, she argues, lies in their understandings of how the mathematical statements work. To grasp Lacan's theorization of the break of modern science — the break in which he situates psychoanalytic discourse — is to recognize Galileo as *replacing* pre-modern nature with a fully mathematized object of science. In other words, as Zupančič writes, "modern science starts when it produces its object," or to put it more strongly, "Galilean science consists in producing its object ('nature') as its own *objective* correlative."[33]

What is at stake, she goes on, is not mediation but replacement. The object of science *is* the mathematical formulas, nothing else; yet it is real because "the (scientific) discourse has consequences. See, for example, landing on the moon." This is not to say there is no reality outside of discourse. As Lacan writes, "Of course I won't dispute this. Nature is there. But what distinguishes it from physics is that it is worth saying something about physics, and that discourse has consequences in it."[34] It is for this reason, as Zupančič points out, that Lacan says that the only possible materialism is dialectical materialism.[35] It is not matter that produces meaning but the impossibly conflictual cut of discourse, which he calls the Real.

Again, what is at stake with Lacan is not representation but replacement: nature is replaced by the (mathematical) letter, a replacement that produces real effects. And although for Meillassoux mathematical formalization and the real are not co-dependent, the relationship is still one of representation. Zupančič describes Meillassoux's notion of mathematical formalization as a kind of net, with the real being "that portion of a substance that does not slip through the net of mathematizable science, but remains caught in it."[36] Lacan's understanding is quite different, as Zupančič says, *"binding the realism of consequences to the modality of the impossible"* as shown in this passage from Seminar XVIII (unpublished in English):

> The articulation, and I mean algebraic articulation, of the semblance — which, as such only involves letters — and its effects, this is the only apparatus by means of which we designate what is real. What is real is what makes/constitutes a hole [*fait trou*] in this semblance, in this articulated semblance that is scientific discourse. Scientific discourse advances without even worrying if it is a semblance or not. What is at stake is simply that its network, its net, its *lattice* as we call it, makes the right holes appear in the right places. It has no other reference but the impossible at which its deductions arrive. This impossible is the real. In physics we only aim at something which is the real by means of a discursive apparatus, insofar as the latter, in its very rigor, encounters the limits of its consistency.[37]

If the impossible is the Real, what to make of the new materialist quest for the great Outside that will redeem philosophical discourse and save the planet? For Zupančič, the great Outside is a fantasy. But not in the sense of a Real that does not exist: "rather, it implies that it is a fantasy in the strict psychoanalytic sense: a screen that conceals the fact that the discursive reality is itself leaking, contradictory, and entangled with the Real as its irreducible other side. That is to say: the great Outside is the fantasy that conceals the Real that is already *right here*."[38]

Critique

Read through the stamp of history, then, both surface reading and the new materialisms can be seen to converge, however inadvertently, with the theoretical readings they wish to leave behind. But convergence does not suture critical fissures, of course, as the convergences between Derrida and Lacan themselves attest. For all the richness with which these two theorists engage with the stamp of history, they diverge in crucial ways with respect to how they read the historical stamp that is the split of meaning and being. And it is precisely their theorizations of sexual difference that offer the sharpest view of that divergence. For, as we have seen, it is in grappling with sexual difference that they explicitly theorize the impossibility of knowing, an impossibility figured by Derrida as undecidability and by Lacan as the Real.

Consider their treatments of the fetish that so stamps modern subjectivity. Both Derrida and Lacan consider fetishism to be a generalized rather than an isolated phenomenon, but in very different ways. Lacan favors Freud's understanding of fetishism as a response to the mother's perceived castration, allowing the fetishist to disavow that castration by means of a substitute. Crucial to Freud's formulation, of course, is his realization that what is involved is not simply the disavowal of castration, but a simultaneous acknowledgment that there is no penis missing. Freud comes late to the realization that the two attitudes persist side by side, that what is involved is not a compromise, as between the ego and the id, but, as he writes in "Splitting of the Ego in the Process of Defence," the simultaneous maintenance of two attitudes achieved "at the price of a rift in the ego which never heals but which increases as time goes on." He continues: "The whole process seems so strange to us because we take for granted the synthetic nature of the processes of the ego. But we are clearly at fault in this. The synthetic function of the ego, though it is of such extraordinary importance, is subject to particular conditions and is liable to a whole number of disturbances."[39]

While Lacan agrees with the phenomenon of disavowal and acknowledgment, what is at stake for him is not the penis but the phallus. What is being disavowed in this formulation, then, is the lack that causes desire, supporting the belief that some presence (i.e. the fetish) produces the desire. And just as Freud increasingly sees simultaneous disavowal and acknowledgment at work in circumstances beyond sexual fetishism per se,[40] so does Lacan extend the operation to perversion in general.

Not surprisingly, Derrida offers a very different reading of Freudian fetishism in *Glas*, that remarkable textual deconstruction of the Hegelian dialectic. There, as in so many of his engagements with psychoanalysis, he frames Freud's views within a deconstructive problematic that finds in them both deconstructive success and failure. Reading Freud's 1927 "Fetishism," Derrida finds there two stances with regard to the fetish: a decidable one and an undecidable one. The decidable is Freud's suggestion that the fetish is a substitute for the mother's missing penis. As Derrida writes:

> Whence ... the *Verleugnung*, the "disavowal" that protects the child against the threat of castration and maintains intact his initial belief (*Glauben*). The fetish erects itself here as a "monument," "a *stigma indelible*," a "sign of triumph." The monumental erection of a supplementary column is a compromise solution, a counterweight solution to balance the "conflict" between the "weight (*Gewicht*)"of the "undesired perception" and "the force of the counter-wish (*Gegenwunsches*)."[41]

This view Derrida labels "strict fetishism," which takes the substitute for the *thing itself*.

It is in the latter part of the essay that Derrida finds a speculative undecidable reading. There, in Freud's discussion of the fetishist whose drawers entirely covered up his genitals, permitting a permanently divided attitude toward the castration of both women and men, Derrida sees an indication of the generalized fetishism that he endorses.

It is true, as Laplanche and Pontalis point out, that in "Fetishism" Freud's interpretation is still ambiguous. On the one hand, they write, he tries to account for the fetishist's inconsistency — his simultaneous disavowal and acknowledgment of feminine castration — "by invoking the process of repression and of compromise-formation between the two conflicting forces; on the other hand, he also shows how the inconsistency actually constitutes a splitting in two (*Spaltung, Zwiespältigkeit*) of the subject."[42] The difference between Laplanche and Pontalis's readings and Derrida's is that the former see Freud's speculations as consistent with his continual reworking of his interpretations, whereas Derrida's sees Freud challenging metaphysical assumptions without ever directly addressing or displacing them.

The difficulty of reading psychoanalysis through a Derridean problematic is particularly clear in the case of fetishism, where what Roudinesco calls Freud's renunciation of the knowledge of being for that of the unconscious is so evident. For Freud, the "thing itself" is of little consequence, and not only because the whole drama of acknowledgment and disavowal circles around a maternal penis that was never there; but because Freud's interpretive work never *rests* with the question of the presence or absence of the object.

The incommensurability of the two problematics is evident as early as "Freud and the Scene of Writing." There Derrida displays very openly where his interest lies: not with reading Freud on his own terms but, as he says to Roudinesco, with finding formulations in support of his own theoretical project. Hence his embrace of much of the Freudian text, and especially *Nachträglichkeit*. But it is in assimilating Freud's work to the problematic of writing that Derrida effectively dismisses the specificity of the Freudian trace.[43] For if the Derridean trace is the absence of presence in the making of meaning, an absence of presence seen in the continual play of différance — in the way the signifier simultaneously differs from and defers the signified — the Freudian trace is something else. Theorizing first in neuro-physiological terms in *Project for a Scientific Psychology*, then four years later in *The Interpretation of Dreams*, Freud aims to grasp the way some perceptual inscriptions seem to appear as conscious "memories" whereas others are unconscious. In the words of François Richard, "The mnemic trace, the notion of unconscious memory that is essential in Freudian theory, results from the inscription upon the psychic apparatus of a perception that is strong enough to cross the barrier of the protective shield.[44] This perception is totally unconscious, whereas the memory of it is conscious." It is thus that "Freud envisaged the psychic apparatus as a system of multiple and complex facilitations of mnemic traces."[45]

Freud saw in his metapsychological construct, Richard continues, "both the complex reality of 'facilitations' in the neurons, which present-day neurobiology would call 'neural networks,' but also a differential system of inscription of perceptual impressions. The postulate of incompatibility between, on the one hand, consciousness and perception, and, on the other hand, the unconscious and the lasting quality of mnemic traces . . . remained intact throughout the developments of his later work." Further elaborating on this question of incompatibility, Richard notes that "in Freud's text the same linguistic root is used for two notions that are contradictory in other languages: the 'mnemic trace' [*Erinnerungsspur*], which is unconscious, and a memory (*Erinnerung*), which is conscious."

Rather than framing Freud's views on the fetish in terms of decidability and undecidability, then, one would do better to begin with his early theories of "screen memories." In Freud's earliest work with analytic patients, he was struck by the way seemingly insignificant memories that appear vivid and persistent can serve to conceal repressed experiences or fantasies. Indeed, in a footnote added in 1920 to the 1905 *Three Essays on the Theory of Sexuality*, Freud draws an explicit connection between fetishism and screen memory. In 1905 he endorses psychologist Alfred Benet's notion that "the choice of a fetish is an after-effect of some sexual impression, received as a rule in early childhood." In 1920 he retracts the endorsement:

> [A]ll of these "early" sexual impressions [in Benet's theory] relate to a time after the age of five or six, whereas psycho-analysis makes it doubtful whether fresh pathological fixations can occur so late as this. The true explanation is that behind the first recollection of the fetish's appearance there lies a submerged

and forgotten phase of sexual development. The
fetish, like a "screen-memory," represents this phase
and is thus a remnant and precipitate of it.[46]

In order to look further at the ways Lacan and Derrida differ in their readings of the stamp of history, I turn to the *other* fetishism, the commodity fetishism that for Marx conveys the secret of the magic of capital.

First, Derrida. As with his reading of Freud, Derrida frames his reading of Marx as a deconstructive radicalization aimed at exposing metaphysical impediments to an otherwise emancipatory project. Unlike his engagements with Freud, however, Derrida refrained from taking on Marx until his 1993 publication of *Specters of Marx*.[47] Although the book was received with enormous critical interest, it did little to alter the terms of debate over the political benefits and dangers of deconstruction. On the one hand, even detractors of Derrida could admire the timing of the book, with its strong criticism of the triumphalist neoliberal celebration of capital's global reach, and its uncharacteristically empirical catalogue of the plagues of the "new world order." On the other hand, Derrida's reading is framed in such a way as to block debate outside the terms of its deconstructive argument. The Marx that appears there speaks to Derrida's critical interests, and those have to do not with Marx's use of the fetish to convey the particular spectral power of capital's form of value, but with what Derrida sees as Marx's failure to maintain a generalized spectrality.

The ghost, that spectral figure that is and is not, shapes Derrida's entire text, joining the critique of metaphysics (hauntology versus ontology) to a call for the messianic without messianism, that is, for the promise of emancipation *à venir* versus the embodied realization of some teleology. Derrida finds that promise embedded in Marx's emancipatory spirit. But he sees it as a promise betrayed by Marx's opting for "ontological presence" in the form of a concrete politics that led through Stalinism to the "death" of Marxism—a "death" in which the ghost of the promise still lives, as Derrida asserts in his call for the messianic *à venir*.

Derrida maintains that it is Marx's "fear of ghosts" that led him to fall on the wrong side of the undecidable. In making the argument he pays a good deal of attention to Marx's critique of Max Stirner (aka Johann Casper Schmidt) in *The German Ideology* where, as in Stirner's work, there is a rich thematic of spectrality. While there is much to be said about Derrida's engagement with that debate,[48] of interest here is how Derrida reads commodity fetishism through the ghostly argument. Indeed, in his reading of Marx's "The Fetishism of the Commodity and the Secret Thereof," the drama resides not in the stealthy cunning of surplus value but in the haunting: "The commodity . . . haunts the thing, its specter is at work in use-value."[49] In other words, Derrida reads Marx as locating the other of capital's spectrality in the realm of use value, which he sees as a pre-deconstructive fall into the ontological.

To have a sense of the gap between Derrida's reading and Marx's text, it is useful to recall Marx's well-known evocation of the commodity as "a very queer thing, abounding in metaphysical subtleties and theological niceties": "So far as it is a value in use, there is nothing mysterious about it, whether we consider it from the point of view that by its properties it is capable of satisfying human wants, or from the point of view that those properties are the product of human labour."[50] He goes on, saying it is clear that

> man changes the forms of the materials of nature
> in such a way as to make them useful to him. The

form of wood, for instance is altered if a table is
made out of it. Nevertheless the table continues to
be wood, an ordinary sensuous thing. But as soon as
it emerges as a commodity, it changes into a thing
which transcends sensuousness. It not only stands
with its feet on the ground but, in relation to all other
commodities, it stands on its head, and evolves out of
its wooden brain grotesque ideas. . . .[51]

Those ideas have to do, of course, with its value, a value determined not by the actual human labor involved in its production, but by abstracted labor-power sold by the wage-laborer as a commodity that produces surplus value for the capitalist. "A commodity is therefore a mysterious thing, simply because in it the social character of men's labour appears to them as an objective character stamped upon the product of that labour; because the relation of the producers to the sum total of their own labor is presented to them as a social relation, existing not between themselves, but between the products of their labour." Hence, again, Marx's famous assessment of commodity fetishism: "There it is a definite social relation between men, that assumes, in their eyes, the fantastic form of a relation between things."[52]

In his reading, Derrida sees "use-value" as something once not haunted, now haunted by commodification, a formulation naively metaphysical in his eyes. For, as he argues, use value and all that goes with it — production, technics, and so forth — are never free of the ghosts of iterability: "If this purity is not guaranteed, then one would have to say that the phantasmagoria began before the said exchange-value, at the threshold of the value of value in general, or that the commodity-form began before the commodity-form, itself before itself."[53]

This argument would have characteristic Derridean

force *if* "use-value" referred to a pure pre-capitalist (and pre-deconstructive) form of use. But this is not how Marx uses the term. Once "use" is figured in the circulation of exchange, its pre-capitalist meanings give way to a meaning legible only through the valuation of exchange. As he makes clear in his detailed reading of the workings of the commodity, "use" and "use-value" are distinctly different terms of signification. If "use-value" benefits from any residual connection to "use," that is all to the capitalist's advantage. But when it comes to the value of a commodity, "use" plays no role.

To produce his deconstructive reading, Derrida casts Marx's text in phenomenological terms. Reading Marx's table, for example, he focuses on its sensuousness: "*Coup de théâtre*: The ordinary sensuous thing is transfigured. . . . This woody and headstrong denseness is metamorphosed into a supernatural thing, a *sensuous non-sensuous* thing. . . . The ghostly schema now appears indispensable. The commodity is a 'thing' without phenomenon, a thing in flight that surpasses the senses."[54]

The problem with the reading is that it occludes Marx's own position on the sensuous, non-sensuous question. For Marx looks not to phenomenology to theorize subjectivity and objectivity, ideality and materiality, but to *praxis*. That sensuous human activity is Marx's concretization of the Hegelian dialectic, without which his theorization of capital's reliance on and foreclosure of abstracted labor-power makes no sense.

In his essay on *Specters of Marx*, titled "Marx's Purloined Letter," Fredric Jameson comments on the question of materialism:

> As for materialism, it ought to be a place in which theory, deconstruction and Marxism meet: a privi-

leged place for theory, insofar as the latter emerges
from a conviction as to the "materiality" of language;
for deconstruction insofar as its vocation has something to do with the destruction of metaphysics; for
Marxism ("historical materialism") insofar as the
latter's critique of Hegel turned on the hypostasis of
ideal qualities and the need to replace such invisible
abstractions by a concrete (that included production
and economics).[55]

Unfortunately, no such meeting occurs in *Specters of Marx*. There, as Jameson says, "under what Derrida stigmatizes as ontology are very much to be ranged all possible conceptions of a materialist philosophy as such."[56] Perhaps, Jameson suggests, we need another way of thinking about materialism:

Rather than conceiving of materialism as a systematic
philosophy, it would seem possible and perhaps more
desirable to think of it as a polemic stance, designed
to organize various anti-idealist campaigns, a proce-
dure of demystification and de-idealization; or else a
permanent linguistic reflexivity. This is, among other
things, why Marxism has never been a philosophy as
such, but rather a "unity-of-theory-and-practice" very
much like psychoanalysis, and for many of the same
reasons.[57]

If it is 1989 that brings Derrida to Marx, for Lacan it is May '68. While his reactions to the May events were mixed, of interest here are the strong theoretical turns he makes beginning in Le *Séminaire, livre XVI, D'un autre à l'Autre* (1968–1969) and in *Seminar Book XVII: The Other Side of Psychoanalysis* (1969–1970). In the first session of *Seminar XVI*, in November 1968, he announces in a discussion of structuralism (with reference to Althusser): "I shall appeal to Marx whose remarks I have had a lot of trouble not introducing earlier, importuned as I have been for a long time about him, in a field in which he is nevertheless perfectly in his place." The place Lacan refers to, where he situates Marx's "essential function," is that of surplus value. And surplus value, he goes on, is homologous with the *objet a*, which means that Marx and psychoanalysis are linked by a structural surplus, for what is "lost" in the process of signification is not really lost but endures in the form of "surplus enjoyment."[58]

While this formulation can seem excessively abstract at first, it gains force if one considers Lacan's development in *Seminar XVII* of the four discourses (of the master, the university, the hysteric, and the analyst), which denote four types of social bond. One popular view of Lacan's turn to Marx and the social bonds sees it as his response to the 1968 student graffiti proclaiming "structures don't take to the street," asserting that social-political signification, like any signification, is a structure of knowing.

What is of particular interest here, in Lacan's treatment of the four discourses, is the question of the subject.[59] Focusing on that question, we see once again the divergences between Lacan and Derrida, this time with consequences for their readings of Marx. Of course, both theorists have as their point of departure the structuralist understanding of language as a chain of differences in which the signifier's value is diachronically constituted as its difference from another signifier, and where meaning is produced not through some intrinsic property but through the workings of the chain. For Derrida, the process of signification always already entails *différance*, the play of the trace. And while Derrida sees language staging the very struggle of "sur-vival" that is life, he finds no such insight in the psychoanalytic subject, which for him is a phenomenal vestige of phallogocentrism.

For Lacan, on the other hand, the formalization of the discursive social bond entails bringing fresh attention to one of his familiar formulations: "the signifier is what represents the subject for another signifier." What is different from earlier discussions of this formulation is that here, in *Seminar XVI*, the focus is on the point of view of the *signifier*: ". . . it is a matter now of referring to fundamental formulas, in particular, that which defines the signifier as being what represents a subject for another signifier. I am surprised that no one has ever yet remarked in connection with this proposition that as a result, as a corollary, a signifier cannot represent itself."[60]

In earlier formulations, Lacan puts the pressure on the unconscious and the constitutive lack in the Other. This is the lack that Zupančič figures as a missing signifier that gives the signifying order its constitutive negativity. Here, where Lacan puts the pressure on the signifier, we see that for him this constitutive negativity is not just an individual matter but a political one, affecting the way discourse forms the social bond. In *Seminar XVII, The Other Side of Psychoanalysis*, he makes this explicit: "The intrusion into the political can only be made by recognizing that the only discourse there is, and not just analytic discourse, is the discourse of *jouissance*, at least when one is hoping for the work of truth from it."[61]

Two terms figure, then, in Lacan's political: *jouissance* and truth. First, *jouissance*. To appreciate what Lacan means by the discourse of *jouissance*, we return to his observation that a signifier cannot represent itself. "When I say that the signifier must be defined as that which represents a subject for another signifier, that means that no one will know anything about it except the other signifier. And the other signifier, it has no head, it is a signifier." What is required, of course, is the subject, but in the process of representation "the subject is there, stifled, effaced, immediately at the same time as it appears."[62]

Produced by one signifier, effaced by another is, of course, the story of the splitting of the subject upon entering the signifying order. But what Lacan insists on here is that it is *also* the story of the signifier: "The subject, in whatever form it is produced in its presence as a subject, cannot rejoin its representative signifier without there being this loss of identity that is, properly speaking, the object a."[63] As Zupančič puts it, the signifier is inadequate to itself, unable "to function 'purely,' without producing a useless surplus." This inadequacy, she says, has two names: "the subject and object a." The subject is what she earlier called the castrating negativity of the signifying order. Here the "subject is the inner gap of the signifier, that which sustains its referential movement." As for the *objet a*, it is "a positive waste that gets produced in this movement and that Lacan calls the surplus enjoyment, making it clear there is no other enjoyment but surplus enjoyment."[64]

When Lacan says, then, that the discourse of *jouissance* is the only discourse of the political, at least if one is looking for truth, we see that the truth we find there is one of impossibility. Signification, or discourse, are constitutively not-whole: "the only way to evoke the truth is by indicating that it is only accessible through a half-saying [*mi-dire*], that it cannot be said completely, in that beyond this half there is nothing to say. That is all that can be said."[65]

If for Derrida the category of the subject belongs to the pre-critical register of metaphysics, for Lacan it performs a function crucial to the reading of a discursive structure and its social bond. As Lacan says in Seminar XVII, in the formalization of a discourse "we encounter an element of impossibility. This is what is at the base, the root, of an effect of structure." It is here that the homologous linkage with

Marx takes on its force in that as Lacan says "the *a* is precisely identifiable with what the thought of a worker, Marx's, produced, namely what was, symbolically and really, the function of surplus value."[66] And of course the homology is doubly enlightening in that for Marx, what produces surplus value, what occupies the structural place of the subject, is not the individual consciousness of the worker, but the *structural function* of class in the form of the proletariat.

What to make of the differences that separate Derrida's and Lacan's readings of the stamp of history? If the challenge for critical reading today is, as Walter Benn Michaels suggests, to grasp "the system itself," namely the full penetration of the logic of capital, how to view this further impasse between Derrida and Lacan?

One can certainly argue that the Lacanian reading of Marx trumps the Derridean, and that the structural subject of the unconscious displaces the deconstructive dismissal of the phenomenal subject. Whatever disciplinary validity there might be in such an argument, however, might also be too tidy. If, as Roudinesco says, Freud renounces the knowledge of being for that of the unconscious, what can be said of this renunciation? A refusal, an abandonment, but also an impossibility. In which case, it might be said that the warring problematics of Derrida and Lacan that produce an undecidable impossible versus the impossibility of the Real, themselves form an impossible knot. And it might also be said that the knot offers a useful insight into the challenges of reading the break of meaning and being: that, to borrow from Luce Irigaray, this impossible is not one.[67]

4
Reading the Feminist Impossible

"Can literary criticism survive the decline of the symptom?" is the question with which Timothy Bewes begins his 2010 essay "Reading against the Grain."[1] We can certainly pose the same question to a feminist theory that has struggled to survive the transactional legibility of neoliberal discourse. Not to all forms of feminist theory, but to the particular form that crossed paths with deconstructive, psychoanalytic, and Marxist critique.

One way of viewing the trajectory of that feminism is to trace the struggles between the problematic of critique and that of identity.[2] In the early years, feminist theory overlapped with and benefitted from civil rights critique. However, both movements soon had to contend with powerful neo-liberal discourses of identity. In the feminist case, ensuing struggles often merged the categories, with debates about critique staged in terms of identity and vice-versa. Such was the case, for example, of the meeting of feminist theory and queer theory, where feminist theory was assigned the terrain of gender (with gender-as-critique devolving into gender-as-identity) and queer theory occupying the register of sexuality.

In the course of such debates, identity categories became increasingly more legible and categories of critique less legible. Such was the fate early on of the critical category of "Woman," which was soon displaced by "women," "women of color," and so forth. That is not to say that considerations of racialization and class were not crucial, but that the familiar legibility of identity, along with the seductions of neoliberal ideology, gradually overpowered considerations of critique. That was the case, for example, of the important insights "womanist" theory offered feminism, a critique that was soon eclipsed by discourses of "diversity." Similarly, "gender," which Scott and Butler launched in different disciplinary contexts as a category of critique, inexorably became the term of identity it is today.

The displacement and dissolution of terms of critique can be seen in part as the very staging of the impossibility constitutive of the feminist project. For to figure "sexual difference" as gendered is precisely to circumscribe difference, that is, to figure "female" in terms of its other. And this conceptual reduction clearly obstructs any engagement with sexual difference as a cut, a division, a gap in the signifying order. Under pressure of identity discourse then, the theoretical category of the gap has no purchase. Instead, male/female is further dispersed as discursively positive sexual multiplicity or as "non-binary" identities.

If feminist impossibility has been richly theorized over the years,[3] why end with yet another call to read the feminist impossible? Perhaps because the very notion of "possible" and "impossible" has a particular resonance today that invites renewed challenge. As Zupančič remarks, in capitalist discourse the "impossible" has been expunged: "Capitalism . . . is above all the discourse of the possible. Its fundamental slogan could be expressed in these terms: 'Impossible is not possible.'"[4] And a discourse in which nothing is impossible is one in which fetishism ceases to be a problem, where the commodity ceases to be the scandalous masking of the exploitation of labor.

This, as Samo Tomšič shows, is just what financial capital claims. In the age of financialization, capital is seen to be a vitalist, autonomous force that produces its own growth without the negativity of surplus value. This financial vitalism should not surprise us, he says, given that "*Geld heckendes Geld*, money-breeding money, as Marx writes, is the main fetishist fantasy that emerges from the autonomy of value, and it is therefore not a surprise that this fantasy of self-engendering stands in the core of all capitalist fetishisms and becomes a driving force of financialization."[5]

Indeed, see Marx's analysis of "The Transformation of Money into Capital":

> [I]n the circulation of M-C-M both the money and the commodity function only as different modes of existence of value itself, the money as its general mode of existence, the commodity as its particular, or so to speak, disguised mode. It is constantly changing from one form into the other, without becoming lost in this movement; it thus becomes transformed into an automatic subject.... In truth, however, value is here the subject of a process in which, while constantly assuming the form in turn of money and commodities, it changes its own magnitude, throws off surplus-value from itself considered as original value, and thus valorizes itself independently. For the movement in the course of which it adds surplus-value is its own movement, its valorization is therefore self-valorization [*Selbstverwertung*]. By virtue of being value, it has ac-

quired the occult ability to add value to itself. It brings forth living offspring, or at least lays golden eggs.[6]

What, then, of feminist impossibility in the regime of finance capital? In Lacan's view, a value producing value identical to itself would be like a signifier representing itself without the structural gap. For Lacan, as Tomšič puts it, capitalist discourse is fraudulent in that it "is grounded on the foreclosure of the impossibility of totalization that marks other discourses, an impossibility that is structurally determined by the fact that the signifiers constitute an open set of differences." In other words, for Lacan, the defining feature of capitalist discourse is "the foreclosure of castration."[7]

To grasp what an affront the capitalist foreclosure of castration is to feminist efforts of all types, it is helpful to recall Lacan's reformulation of "castration." If sex is the very incompleteness of being, the constitutive short-circuiting of the vital and psychic orders, "castration" performs that short-circuiting in the institution of the subject in the field of the Other. And if "castration" and "phallus" retain their masculine specificity, it is because in Lacan's formulation the symbolic field is not neutral, but pressingly phallocentric — with, as its master signifier, a sham phallus that works everywhere to disavow castration.

It is not news that financial capital aims to close its own constitutive structural gap with, among other means, the discursive help of algorithms and technology. What is striking, perhaps, is that late capitalist discourse infects even conventional critical discourses. Of course, in some modes of criticism, the relationship between critique and the object of critique can be uncomfortably close, with what seems like critique turning out to be description. See, for example, Michaels's discussion of the way an earlier art historical critique that aimed to oppose commodification actually mirrored it:

"Think of the critique of the artist's intentionality and the celebration of indeterminacy, of the artist's willingness to give up control of the work, etc.," all descriptions of the art commodity that exists only to be sold.[8]

The post-critical turn is different, however. There, in many cases the critical discourse has the stated aim of displacing, closing, or repairing the gaps that enable critique. The temptation to do so can be strong. To yield to the lure of a discourse that aims to expunge the impossible is to enjoy the pleasure of collective endorsement, of legibility, the known. But that pleasure can come at a cost. A discourse in which nothing is impossible is one in which there is all pleasure and no *jouissance*; and the problem with that, Zupančič says, is that one is deprived of the very gaps that structure the social bond, the very gaps of contradiction that enable political change. Moreover, it is not as if impossibility completely disappears, she comments, "it just keeps reappearing in new, unexpected configurations."[9]

Feminist critical reading turns out, then, to have renewed importance in this age, if only to remind us that the very possibility for change is impossibility. Indeed, this seems a propitious time for reading the feminist impossible. I call such a reading "feminist" because it resists the phallic erasure of castration; "impossible" because the reader is in the position Barbara Johnson evokes: "the place where representation would be understood if there were any such thing as a place beyond representation." To be such a reader in the structural gap of the signifying order can be to read both the fraudulent and the powerful effects of structures and their gaps. Such a reading can be even better than reading for closure; it can, in Zupančič's words "bind the realism of consequences to the modality of the impossible."

Coda

What Eve Sedgwick disliked about "paranoid reading" was that it overwhelms the text, "blotting out any sense of the possibility of alternative ways of understanding things *or* things to understand." She worried that if it persisted as a mode of reading it could "impoverish the gene pool of literary-critical perspectives and skills. The trouble with a shallow gene pool, of course, is its diminished ability to respond to environmental (e.g., political) change." What Sedgwick was calling for, in other words, was *more* critique.[1]

In the decades since Sedgwick expressed her concern about the survival of critical reading, the stakes have grown only higher. There is still reason to worry that pedagogies of reading continue to promote texts that are overwhelmed by the already-known, though now a more dangerous thematically driven already-known rather than a theoretical one. There is even more reason to fear larger institutional failures to support both critical thinking and critical thinkers. But against that grim background and against all odds, it is emboldening to be able to say that Sedgwick need not have worried about the critical gene pool. Here, following, are examples from a few readers who demonstrate that truth.

Each reading has a frame that seems to invite the legibility that grounds its field of inquiry. But in doing the work of not knowing, each reading displaces legible expectations, not in order to offer alternative closure but to open up the productive impossibility of interpretive certainty.

The "appeal" in "2002: A Reading Appeal" is addressed to those who confront survivor testimonies.[2] *What if* the appalling acts of violence are experienced by the perpetrators as the most extreme forms of sexual pleasure, bringing to life what Jacqueline Rose calls "the obscenity of the unconscious"? In *Females*, there is no "other sex" that one can occupy, no "non-binary" multiplicity. There is only the universally despised and universally desired category of female, that is to say, the impossible structure of human sexuality.[3]

If questions of sexuality so grippingly stage the impossibility of knowing, they are, of course, not the only questions that call for feminist resistance to phallic closure. In reading modalities of Black subjectivity, *None Like Us* turns away from the collective "we" of Black history that holds out "a sense of loss in the hope of retrieval" for an impossible rhetoric based on "knowing what withholds itself from the possibility of being known."[4] And the fictional animals in *Behold an Animal* evoke not some positivity to be thought with and against human positivity but rather — a bit like Zupančič's "missing signifier" that produces a gap in the signifying order — something missing in the story.[5]

Sexual Violence

The archive of the 2002 Gujarat riots literally repeats what it cannot read, Samia Vasa warns. What if feminist readings of the archive are so identified with the Muslim victims, and the archive "so driven in the name of justice that it cannot read the very thing it documents over and over: the fantastic contours of Hindu pleasure." What if stabbing a terrified child with a sword and tossing her into the fire; hacking open a pregnant belly and burning first fetus then mother; pouring petrol in the throat of a six-year old boy then igniting it; what if all that were the best of joyful fun and the greatest of sexual pleasures. What if rumors that cast such pleasure as the justified revenge for the fanaticized rape of Hindu women are *known* to be true, "what kind of knowing is this?" Vasa asks.[6] And what if really reading the archive, what if inhabiting the negative force of sexuality were the only way of "unlocking the rapeful subject," even "if there never was any place from which one could see one's own self watching what was happening."

Black Studies

Stephen Best views the reading of black history in two ways, involving two types of scholarly sacrifice, both "torqued . . . by race and the ghost of slavery," but distinctly different. The first, a "melancholic sacrifice," is a kind of debt the reader owes to the other, who does not exist though the reader does, a debt executed "not in living, but in reanimating the other." With the second "astringent sacrifice," the reader must acknowledge that "were it not for the other's obliteration, I would not exist." Given that the "melancholy historicism" of the first dominates readings of the black archive, Best calls for a shift from the *historical* mode that keeps reintroducing loss, to a *rhetorical* one that "succeeds in failing." He views the melancholy historical mode, which cannot let go of what is not there, as, in Walter Benn Michaels's words, hypostasizing "the absence of evidence as the evidence of absence." On the other hand, the rhetorical mode, he writes, citing Michel de Certeau, "'succeeds in failing' much like the tropes of metalepsis and litotes, which involve a negation or an awareness of moving 'from a *can not say* . . . to a *can say* . . . by way of a *can say nothing*.'"[7]

For his readings, Best takes as his rhetorical model the work from which his book's title is drawn: David Walker's 1833 *Appeal to the Coloured Citizens of the World*, an appeal that like a litote, "bears a set of alternatives that it also liquidates": ". . . we (coloured people of these United States) are the most degraded, wretched, and abject set of beings that ever lived since the world began; and I pray God that none like us may ever live again until time shall be no more."[8]

Trans Studies

The reader cannot not be trapped in the relentless logic of *Females*. It is the unforgiving logic that Andrea Long Chu so admires in Valerie Solanas, of *SCUM Manifesto* fame, for whom the "simple greatest hoax in the history of human civilization was the simple idea that men are men."[9] *Females'* logic resides in an address to you the reader that mirrors the provocation of castration. That is to say: "Everyone is female, and everyone hates it," meaning *Females* is "simply restating something psychoanalytically uncontroversial — namely, that castration happens *on both sides*." Thus, being female and hating it is not about being a woman or a man, but about "having someone else do your desiring for you, at your own expense." It is not about anatomy or genetics, but rather "the one and only structure of human consciousness. To be is to be female: the two are identical." Gender is, then, the form "internalized misogyny" takes in any given case, in that in making you an object, gender "expresses, in every case, the desires of another." As for feminism, "Politics is, in its essence, anti-female." That is because "politics begins, in every case, from the optimistic belief that *another sex is possible*. This is the root of all political consciousness: the dawning realization that one's desires are not one's own, that one has become a vehicle for someone else's ego; in short, that one is female, but wishes it were not so."

But even if there is no escaping the logic of *Females*, there is more to the story. Desire may come from the outside "like a tongue of fire, or an infection — or a mental illness" so that "no one in their right mind would want to be female" — "except that some at least are drawn to being women" (women being females' "select delegates"). It may be that pussy envy is "the universal desire atop which [penis envy] develops as a reaction formation: Everyone does their best to want power, because deep down, no one wants it at all." What one wants, Chu writes, "is to become what someone else wants," which is to be female, which makes autogynephilia *"the basic structure of all human sexuality."*[10]

Animals

Neither the "behold" nor the "animal" in Thangam Ravindranathan's *Behold an Animal* meets what one might consider reasonable readerly expectations. The experience of the book is better announced by the full title: *Behold an Animal. Four Exorbitant Readings*. And as exorbitant as the readings are in their resistance to interpretive closure, they are thus because the animal in question fails to be contained by any naturalist assumptions. "An altogether more unsettling experience of reading opens up when we resist the naturalist temptation and defer 'recognition'," Ravindranathan writes. The animal we behold in the readings is a *something missing* — in the human, in the real — as in Eric Chevillard's *Without the Orangutan*.[11] There, in a world where the orangutan no longer exists, the very meanings and pacts that hold nature and history together collapse. "What long made possible, or at least invisible, a contract — between language and animal bodies [*signe* and *singe*] — which now, on the death of the last orangutans, should lie so exposed and undone?" Ravindranathan questions. Following readings that cannily and uncannily trace that question in the folds and figures of the texts of Chevillard, La Fontaine, and Poe, Ravindranathan offers in response: "Inextricably exorbitant to itself, the human needed the orangutan in order to better resemble itself."

The response continues throughout and in the Epilogue, which evokes the scandal and paradox of the *nothing* that "ruins every economy": "the fact that even as within our inhabitable reality everything is exchangeable, reality itself can be exchanged only for nothing. . . . a place where the production of meaning and value must implode, for it reaches its outside." "According to Baudrillard," she continues, "human economies and systems share as their ultimate drive the hunt to exterminate this Nothing — which he also calls the Inhuman."[12] In the course of writing this book," Ravindranathan reflects, "I came to think of animals as marking gaps, thresholds, tricks, twists, vanishing points that stories or thought might usually cover up or leave unthought. . . . Placeholders for bits of thought and life difficult to think, they were perhaps figures for our relationship with nothing, and, by that impossible measure, with everything."[13]

Acknowledgments

If I were to thank all the brilliant friends and colleagues whose work I have learned from over the years, the list would be longer than this short book. So, I will limit my grateful acknowledgments to those who offered helpful comments on this project: Joan Scott, Ann du Cille, Ona Nierenberg, Lynne Joyrich, Ellen Rooney, and Denise Davis. My gratitude as well to Suzanne Stewart-Steinberg and Leela Gandhi for their strong leadership of the Pembroke Center in these challenging times; and to my co-editors of *differences*, Ellen Rooney and Denise Davis, for continuing to make the work of the journal so enjoyable. I am very fortunate to have had the editorial guidance of the discerning Tom Lay. And I am grateful to Anna Steinberg, who took time from her real life as an artist and critic to lend me invaluable editing and computer assistance.

My deepest gratitude is to my dear friend Joan Wallach Scott. Thinking and working with her since we met some four decades ago at Brown has been, and continues to be, an incredible pleasure. I can't imagine any of it without her. This book, however modest, is for her.

Notes

Prologue: Why read the impossible now?

1. Recounted in François Dosse, *History of Structuralism, Vol. 2: The Sign Sets, 1967–Present*, trans. Deborah Glassman (Minneapolis and London: University of Minnesota Press, 1997), 122.

2. Elisabeth Roudinesco, *Jacques Lacan*, trans. Barbara Bray (New York: Columbia University Press, 1997), 341.

3. *The Seminar of Jacques Lacan, Book VII: The Other Side of Psychoanalysis*, trans. Russell Grigg (New York and London: W.W. Norton & Co. 2007), 207.

4. Jacques Lacan, "The Instance of the Letter in the Unconscious," *Écrits*, trans. Bruce Fink (New York and London: W.W. Norton & Co. 1966), 417.

5. Trans-exclusionary radical feminists. Where academic feminists once asked "what is a woman?" in an effort to grasp the impenetrable knot of misogyny, today the question is an identitarian one with concrete effects, as in the adoption of the term "pregnant person."

6. Eve Kosofsky Sedgwick, "Paranoid Reading and Reparative Reading, or You're So Paranoid, You Probably Think This Essay

Is about You" was published in 2003 in *Touching Feeling: Affect, Pedagogy, Performativity*. An earlier version appeared as part of the introduction to Sedgwick, ed., *Novel Gazing: Queer Readings in Fiction* (Durham & London: Duke University Press, 1997).

7. Sedgwick, 141. Sedgwick's reference to reality as mediated by television is, of course, prescient. See Lynne Joyrich's analyses of the televisual nature of the social field in "TV Trumps," in *Unwatchable*, eds. Nicholas Baer, Maggie Hennefeld, Laura Horek, and Gunnar Iverssen (New Brunswick, NJ: Rutgers University Press, 2019).

8. Sedgwick, 141.

9. Bruno Latour, "Why Has Critique Run out of Steam? From Matters of Fact to Matters of Concern," *Critical Inquiry* 30 (Winter 2004): 226–28.

10. A single example from the field of semantics is entertaining. In English, as in some other languages, the word for a husband who has lost a wife can only be formed from the word designating the reverse: widower<widow. A search for synonyms of "widower" immediately reaches a dead-end of catachresis.

11. See Joan W. Scott's *Only Paradoxes to Offer: French Feminisms and the Rights of Man* (Cambridge, MA and London: Harvard University Press, 1996) for a reading of the impossible choices faced by feminists in French liberal democracy from the Revolution through enfranchisement in 1944 and beyond.

12. Stephen Best and Sharon Marcus, "Surface Reading: An Introduction," *Representations* 108 (Fall 2009).

13. Barbara Johnson, "Writing," *Critical Terms for Literary Study*, eds. Frank Lentricchia and Thomas McLaughlin (Chicago and London: The University of Chicago Press, 1995), 40.

14. Moreover, post-critique itself has tended to fall on either side of the divide between knowing and being. On the one hand, there is a focus on the experiential, as in much of popular affect theory; on the other, a turn to the "material"; or, as in speculative realism, an effort to dismantle Kantianism in service of the real.

15. Alexander G. Weheliye, "Black Studies and Black Life," *The Black Scholar* 44, no. 2 (2014): 5.

16. Frank B. Wilderson III, *Red, White & Black: Cinema and the Structure of U.S. Antagonisms* (Durham & London: Duke University Press) was published in 2010. #Black Lives Matter was founded in 2013 by Alicia Garza, Patrisse Cullors, and Opel Tometi.

17. Frank Wilderson discussion with Jocelyn Burrell, UCI Illuminations, February 3, 2021, YouTube.

It is noteworthy that it was after the dismantling of the radical Left and the violent "neutralization" of black radicals by COINTELPRO, that the discourse of human rights was broadly propagated in the US. Although the Universal Declaration dates from 1948, it was during Carter's administration that the discourse was energetically promoted. COINTELPRO was shut down in 1972; Carter took office in 1977.

18. Attentive to the demands of historical specificity, Wilderson cites among others David Eltis's demonstration that the importation of African slaves to the Americas was much more costly to the Europeans than the importation of the white underclass would have been, and Patterson, who distinguishes between the chattel slavery of traditional cultures and that of the Americas. See David Eltis, "Europeans and the Rise and Fall of African Slavery in the Americas: An Interpretation," *American Historical Review* 98, no. 5 (1993); and Orlando Patterson, *Slavery and Social Death: A Comparative Study* (Cambridge: Harvard University Press, 1982).

19. Wilderson, *Red, White & Black*, 38. See Shaul Magid, "Judeopessimism: On Antisemitism and Afropessimism," Ayin Press, 2021, https://ayinpress.org.

20. Wilderson, *Red, White & Black*, 18.

21. Robert Nichols, *The World of Freedom: Heidegger, Foucault, and the Politics of Historical Ontology* (Stanford: Stanford University Press, 2014), 58. Cited in Jared Sexton, "Afro-Pessimism: The Unclear Word," *Rhizomes: Cultural Studies in Emerging Knowledge* 29 (2016): footnote 6. (http://www.rhizomes.net).

22. Wilderson, *Red, White & Black*, 58

23. Sexton, "Afro-Pessimism," paragraph 14.

24. Sexton, paragraph 16.

25. Thus it is, for example, that Hortense Spillers—whose work is central to the Afro-pessimist argument and who warned early on about the limits of empiricism and the need for psychoanalysis in black studies—can say she is not an Afro-pessimist. See Spillers's "AfroPessimism and Its Others," New School, YouTube, June 9, 2021; and "'Whatcha Gonna Do?' Revisiting 'Mama's Baby, Papa's Maybe: An American Grammar Book'": A Conversation with Hortense Spillers, Saidiya Hartman, Farah Jasmine Griffin, Shelley Eversley, & Jennifer L. Morgan, *Women's Studies Quarterly* 35, nos. 1&2 (2007).

Similarly, Saidiya Hartman, whose work is central to the argument and who suggested the name "Afro-pessimism" to Wilderson, has a reading practice very different from his. Where Wilderson frames Afro-pessimism as something of a manifesto—"how we cannot think"—Hartman sees her work as reading the *unthought*, saying of *Scenes of Subjection*: "I think of the book as an allegory; its argument is a history of the present."

See "The Position of the Unthought: An Interview with Saidiya Hartman Conducted by Frank B. Wilderson III," *Qui Parle* 13, no. 2 (2003):190.

26. Hortense J. Spillers, "Mama's Baby, Papa's Maybe: An American Grammar Book," *Black, White, and in Color* (Chicago and London: The University of Chicago Press, 2003), 206. Originally published in *diacritics* 17, no. 2 (1987).

27. Judith Butler, *Gender Trouble: Feminism and the Subversion of Identity* (New York and London, Routledge, 1990), 33, cited in Kalpana Seshadri-Crooks, *Desiring Whiteness: A Lacanian Analysis of Race* (New York and London: Routledge, 2000), 136; and by Wilderson, *Red, White & Black*, 310.

28. Wilderson, 314.

29. Wilderson, 86.

30. Wilderson, 68–69.

"Empty speech" refers to Lacan's imaginary register, the register of signification, in which the ego finds its counterpart; "full speech" to the symbolic register, the register of meaning (*sens*), closer to the "true" work of unconscious desire. Note that Lacan did not play on the opposition "full" and "empty" after 1955.

31. Wilderson, 73.

32. David S. Marriott, *Lacan Noir: Lacan and Afro-pessimism* (Switzerland: Palgrave Macmillan, 2021), 146.

33. "This is why," he goes on, "the task of analysis is not to cure, as if chasing the hare could distract us from the miseries pursuing us, or the gratuitous violence by which we enjoy the hunt rather than the capture." Marriott, *Lacan Noir*, 148.

34. Marriott, 9.

35. Marrriott, 6. In her early argument for the need of a psychoanalytic perspective in black studies, Spillers expresses a different but resonant view: "In short, how might psychoanalytic theories speak about "race" as self-consciously assertive reflexivity, and how might "race" expose the gaps that psychoanalytic theories awaken?" in "'All the Things You Could Be by Now, if Sigmund Freud's Wife Was Your Mother': Psychoanalysis and Race," *Black and White and in Color*, 376. First published in *boundary* 2 23, no. 3 (1996). See also Spillers's "Time and Crisis: Questions for Psychoanalysis and Race," *Journal of French and Francophone Philosophy* 26, no 2 (2018).

36. Marriott, *Lacan Noir*, 170–71.

37. Patrice D. Douglass, "Black Feminist Theory for the Dead and Dying," *Theory and Event* 21, no. 1 (2018); *All the Women Are White, All the Blacks Are Men, But Some of Us Are Brave: Black Women's Studies*, ed. Gloria T. Hull, Patricia Bell Scott, and Barbara Smith (Old Westbury, N.Y.: The Feminist Press, 1982).

38. Gaines was murdered by police dispatched to her house for failure to appear in traffic court. In an earlier traffic stop, she was arrested, with her five-year old in the back seat, when filming the police with her phone.

39. Douglass, "Black Feminist Theory," 110, citing Sylvia Wynter, "Unsettling the Coloniality of Being/Power/Truth/Freedom: Towards the Human, After Man, Its Overrepresentation," *CR: The New Centennial Review* 3, no. 3 (2003): 313.

40. Douglass, 116.

41. Douglass, 116.

42. Douglass, 117. Douglass is citing Wilderson's words as to what Afro-pessimism does not aim to do (Wilderson, *Red, White & Black*, 58).

43. It is telling that in his incisive "Afro-pessimism: The Unclear Word," Sexton's turn to the particular violence black women experience is marked by a literal break in the text, after which he points to #SayHerName as a *corrective* to #BlackLivesMatter. "How, then, did a black radical political-intellectual project generated largely by the labor of black queer women and centrally by the discourse of black feminist and queer theory become associated, again and again and still, with a masculinist and heteronormative popular reception?" (Sexton, "Afro-Pessimism," paragraph 22).

44. See Joan W. Scott, "Gender: A Useful Category of Historical Analysis," *Gender and the Politics of History* (New York: Columbia University Press, 1988), first published in the *American Historical Review* 91, no. 5 (1986); and Judith Butler, *Gender Trouble*.

45. Joan W. Scott, *Gender and the Politics of History*, Revised Edition (New York: Columbia University Press, 1999), xi.

46. See special issue "*More Gender Trouble: Feminism Meets Queer Theory.*" *differences* 6, nos. 2–3 (1994). Rpt. with revisions in *Feminism Meets Queer Theory*, eds. Elizabeth Weed and Naomi Schor (Bloomington and Indianapolis: Indiana University Press, 1997).

For the critical convergence of Afro-pessimism and queer theory, see Lee Edelman, *Bad Education: Why Queer Theory Teaches Us Nothing* (Durham and London: Duke University Press, 2023).

47. *Female Subjects in Black and White: Race, Psychoanalysis, Feminism*, eds. Elizabeth Abel, Barbara Christian, Helene Moglen (Berkley, Los Angeles, and London: University of California Press, 1997), 1.

48. Ann du Cille, "The Occult of True Black Womanhood:

Critical Demeanor and Black Feminist Studies," *Female Subjects in Black and White*, 21, 26. Originally published in *Signs* 19, no. 3 (1994).

49. The value of the exchange is determined by the cost of labor-time to produce the commodity, not from concrete human labor, but from abstracted labor time measured in terms of its monetary value. So, commodity object is exchanged for the price of commodity labor-time.

50. du Cille, "The Occult of True Black Womanhood," 34.

51. du Cille, 49.

52. Karl Marx, *Capital: A Critical Analysis of Capitalist Production*, Vol. 1, ed. Frederick Engels, trans. Samuel Moore and Edward Aveling (New York: International Publishers, 2003), 504.

53. In chapter VII of *Capital*, Marx writes: "One thing . . . is clear—Nature does not produce on the one side owners of money or commodities, and on the other men possessing nothing but their own labour-power. The relation has no natural basis, neither is its social basis one that is common to all historical periods. It is clearly the result of a past historical development, the product of many economic revolutions, of the extinction of a whole series of older forms of social production.

So, too, the economic categories, already discussed by us, bear the stamp of history. Definite historical conditions are necessary that a product become a commodity." *Capital*, 166.

54. See Section IV, "The Fetishism of Commodities and the Secret Thereof."

55. Louis Althusser and Etienne Balibar, *Reading Capital*, trans. Ben Brewster (London and New York: Verso, 1970).

56. Michel Foucault, *The Order of Things: An Archaeology of the Human Sciences*, trans. Alan Sheridan (New York: Vintage Books, 1970).

57. Michel Foucault, *The Birth of Biopolitics: Lectures at the Collège de France 1978–79*, ed. Michel Senellart, trans. Graham Burchell (New York: Palgrave Macmillan, 2008), 218.

58. Foucault, 218–19. Cited as a "fairly free reformulation" of

Hayek's thoughts in the postscript to *The Constitution of Liberty*, "Why I am Not a Conservative," 398–99.

59. Bill Readings, *The University in Ruins* (Cambridge: Harvard University Press, 1996).

60. Although discussions of "post-identity" and the exhaustion of identity as a critical category began around the time of post-critique, the politics of post-identity had yet to take to the streets. See, for example, "The Future of Criticism — A *Critical Inquiry* Symposium," *Critical Inquiry* 30 (Winter 2004).

61. See Walter Benn Michaels and Adolph Reed Jr, *No Politics but Class Politics*, ed. Anton Jäger and Daniel Zamora (New York: Columbia University Press, 2023); Wendy Brown, *States of Injury: Power and Freedom in Late Modernity* (Princeton: Princeton University Press, 1995).

62. Alenka Zupančič, *Ethics of the Real: Kant and Lacan* (London and New York: Verso, 2000), 225, citing *The Seminar of Jacques Lacan, Book VII: The Ethics of Psychoanalysis* (London: Routledge, 1992), 187.

Hence Afro-pessimism's refusal of the neoliberal discourses and practices of diversity, multiculturalism, and multiracism. As Wilderson writes, "Black people embody . . . a meta-aporia for political thought and action." in "Without Priors," *The Big No*, ed. Keenan Ferguson (Minneapolis and London: University of Minnesota Press, 2021), 89. See Jared Sexton's *Amalgamation Schemes*. (Minneapolis: Minneapolis University Press, 2008).

63. Primož Krašovek, "Neoliberal Epistemology — From the Impossibility of Knowing to Human Capital," *Philozofija I Društvo* 24, no 4 (2013). Hayek, Polanyi, and Drucker were liberal intellectuals whose rejections of social planning and embrace of the free market were responses to the rise of fascism and totalitarianism. Hayek, for one, firmly insisted he was not a conservative.

64. Krašovec, 66.
65. Krašovec, 66.
66. Krašovec, 67.

67. Best and Marcus, "Surface Reading," 16. For a different reading of Stephen Best, see the Coda.
68. Alenka Zupančič, *What Is Sex?* (Cambridge, MA and London: The MIT Press, 2017), 41.

1. States of Impasse

1. Jacqueline Rose, "Donald Trump's victory is a disaster for modern masculinity," *The Guardian*, Nov. 15, 2016.
2. Luce Irigaray, *An Ethics of Sexual Difference*, trans. Carolyne Burke and Gillian C. Gill (Ithaca, NY: Cornell University Press, 1993), 5.
3. For a trans theoretical reading that celebrates the profound uncertainty of gender, see the Coda.
4. Barbara Johnson, "Women and Allegory," *The Wake of Deconstruction* (Cambridge, MA: Blackwell Publishers, 1994). Johnson adopts the formulation "as a" from Nancy K. Miller's *Getting Personal* (New York: Routledge, 1991).
5. Paul de Man, *Blindness and Insight* (Minneapolis, University of Minnesota Press, 1983), 207; cited in Johnson, 62–63.
6. Derrick Bell, *And We Are Not Saved: The Elusive Quest for Racial Justice* (New York: Basic Books, 1987).
7. On the page titled "Sexual Orientation and Gender Identity Definitions" of the Human Rights Campaign, "sexual orientation" is given an identificatory definition: "an inherent or immutable enduring emotional, romantic or sexual attraction to other people." https://www.hrc.org/resources/sexual-orientation-and-gender-identity-terminology-and-definitions
8. Eloise Brook, "Trans, transgender, cisgender: we are what we name ourselves," The Conversation, August 11, 2014, http://theconversation.com. One needs to add to Brook's account the current importance of preferred pronouns.
9. Johnson, "Women and Allegory," 68–73.
10. The one term that evokes some contractual discussion in Brook's post is "cisgender," which, she writes "pushes

those critical of trans people to argue in terms of gender majorities and minorities — and not in terms of legitimacy and deviancy." It is noteworthy, however, that the term "cisgender" emerged in contrast to "trans" rather than as an expression of felt identity.

11. Johnson, "Women and Allegory," 72.

12. Best, Stephen and Sharon Marcus, "Surface Reading: An Introduction," *Representations* 108 (Fall 2009): 9.

13. Marx, *Capital: A Critical Analysis of Capitalist Production*, Vol. 1, ed. Frederick Engels, trans. Samuel Moore and Edward Aveling. New York: International Publishers, 2003, 77.

14. Sharon Marcus, Heather Love, and Stephen Best, "Building a Better Description," *Representations* 135 (Summer 2016).

2. Reading Sexual Difference

1. In this respect *m/f* resembled *Feminist Studies*, a more orthodox socialist feminist journal begun by a feminist collective in New York in 1973. The liberal feminist journal *Signs* began publication with The University of Chicago Press in 1975.

Citations from *m/f* editorial statements refer to the republication of those statements in the volume dedicated to the journal, *The Woman in Question: m/f*, edited by Parveen Adams and Elizabeth Cowie in 1990. Adams and Cowie, the journal's original editors, were joined in the second issue of the journal by Beverly Brown. Rosalind Coward, who facilitated the planning and publishing of the journal, signed the first editorial statement, along with Adams and Cowie.

2. Adams, Parveen and Elizabeth Cowie, eds. *The Woman in Question: m/f*, (Cambridge, MA: The MIT Press, 1990), 38: issue 11/12, 1986.

3. Parveen and Cowie, 34: issue 4, 1980.

4. "Clearly the Women's Movement is not a coherent expression of oppressed womanhood or universal condition, but itself a system of alliances between groupings of interests of

mothers, workers, lesbians, battered wives, etc., and this does produce the problem of the basis for these alliances, a problem already recognized within socialist feminism. Once this is recognized, it is surprising that the very possibility of using the term 'woman' across a range of constructions is itself raised as an insuperable problem unique to m/f," *The Woman in Question*, 33: issue 4, 1980.

For some predecessors to intersectional theory in the U.S., see The Combahee River Collective, *A Black Feminist Statement* (1977) in *All the Women Are White, All the Blacks are Men, But Some of Us Are Brave*; and *This Bridge Called My Back: Writings by Radical Women of Color*, ed. Cherríe Moraga and Gloria E Anzaldúa (Watertown, MA: Persephone Press, 1981).

5. "If possession is usually thought of as the more or less absolute control of a unitary thing by a unified subject, then we are challenging all three of these elements," Parveen and Cowie, 28: issue 3 1979.

6. Parveen and Cowie, 29: issue 3 1979.

7. Parveen and Cowie, 36–37: issue 5/5 1981.

8. Parveen and Cowie, 38–39: issue 11/12 1986.

9. See the special issue "Literature and Psychoanalysis. The Question of Reading: Otherwise," ed. Shoshana Felman, *Yale French Studies* 55/56 (1977).

10. Jacques Derrida, *Dissemination*, trans. and introduction, Barbara Johnson (Chicago, The University of Chicago Press, 1981), ix.

11. Jacqueline Rose, "Donald Trump's victory is a disaster for modern masculinity," *The Guardian*, Nov. 15, 2016

12. Jacques Derrida and Christie V. McDonald, Interview, "Choreograhies," special issue "Cherchez la Femme: Feminist Critique/Feminist Text," *diacritics* 12, no. 2 (1982): 76.

13. *The Seminar of Jacques Lacan: On Feminine Sexuality, The Limits of Love and Knowledge, Éncore*, trans. Bruce Fink (New York and London: W.W. Norton & Co., 1998), 79–80.

14. Elisabeth Roudinesco, *Jacques Lacan*, trans. Barbara Bray (New York: Columbia University Press, 1997), 527.

15. François Dosse, *History of Structuralism, Vol. 1*, trans. Deborah Glassman (Minneapolis and London: University of Minnesota Press, 1997), 319.

16. Plus, in 1966 alone, the year that Dosse dubs the "annus mirabilis," there were major publications by, among others, Foucault, Barthes, Griemas, Todorov, Genette, Benveniste, Macheray, and Canguilhem.

17. It is customary to retain the French title because of the importance for Derrida of the "postal principle," which will be discussed presently. The debate between the two theorists is textually one-sided since Lacan never formally addressed Derrida's criticisms, which is not to say that he did not respond. See, for example his "Lituraterre," in *Littérature*, no. 3 (1971). Elizabeth Roudinesco, Benoît Peeters, and others provide colorful reports of Lacan's informal engagements with Derrida. See Peeters, *Derrida: A Biography*, trans. Andrew Brown (Cambridge U.K. and Malden, MA: Polity Press, 2013).

18. Barbara Johnson, "Translator's Introduction," in Derrida, Jacques, *Dissemination* trans. Barbara Johnson (Chicago, The University of Chicago Press, 1981), vii.

19. Jacques Derrida, "Letter to a Japanese Friend," *Psyche: Inventions of the Other, Vol. II*, eds. Peggy Kamuf and Elizabeth Rottenberg (Stanford: Stanford University Press, 2008), 5.

20. Jacques Derrida, *Speech and Phenomena and Other Essays on Husserl's Theory of Signs* (Evanston, IL: Northwestern University Press, 1973), 156.

21. Jacques Derrida, "Différance," *Margins of Philosophy*, trans. Alan Bass (Chicago: The University of Chicago Press, 1982), 9.

22. Jacques Derrida, "Signature, Event, Context," *Limited Inc.*, trans. Samuel Weber and Jeffrey Mehlman (Evanston, IL: 1988).

23. Johnson, "Translator's Introduction," xxxii.

24. Derrida, *Dissemination*, 220. It is in this context that Johnson writes "The passage from Plato's *antre* to Mallarmé's *entre* is thus a passage from ontological semantics to undecidable syntax," xxviii.

25. Derrida, "Choreographies," 80.
26. Derrida, 72.
27. Derrida, 70.
28. Anne Berger, "Sexing Differances," special issue "Derrida's Gift," *differences* 16, no. 3 (2005): 53.
29. Berger, 66, footnote 7.
30. Jacques Derrida, *Learning to Live Finally: The Last Interview*, trans. Michael Nass and Pascale-Anne Brault (Brooklyn and London: Melville House, 2007), 26.
31. Derrida, 51–52.
32. Frida Saal, "Lacan ◊ Derrida," transcription from a speech at the Tenth Symposium of the Fundacion Mexicana de Psicoanálisis, on *Writing and Psychoanalysis*, February 1994.
33. See Derrida, *Speech and Phenomena and Other Essays on Husserl's Theory of Signs*.
34. David Roden, "The Subject," *Understanding Derrida: An Invitation to Philosophy*, eds. Jack Reynolds and Jonathan Roffe (London and New York: Continuum, 2004), 94.
35. Jacques Derrida, *Of Grammatology*, trans. Gayatri Chakravorty Spivak (Baltimore and London: The Johns Hopkins University Press, 1976), 70–71.
36. Freud worked with the model or fiction of the *psychic or mental apparatus*, and within that of systems and agencies, which serve as a powerful critique of the notion of the unified subject of consciousness. His first model focuses on the differentiations among the unconscious, preconscious, and conscious systems; his second model differentiates the three agencies of id, ego, and super-ego.
37. Adrian Johnston writes: "the Lacanian Symbolic is initially theorized on the basis of resources provided by structuralism. Tied to natural languages as characterized by Saussure and specific post-Saussurians, this register also refers to the customs, institutions, laws, mores, norms, practices, rituals, rules, traditions, and so on of cultures and societies (with these things being entwined in various ways with language). . . . This non-natural universe is an elaborate set of inter-subjective and

trans-subjective contexts into which individual human beings are thrown at birth (along the lines of Heideggerian *Geworfenheit*), a pre-existing order preparing places for them in advance and influencing the vicissitudes of their ensuing lives" ("The Symbolic," Lacan.com).

38. Lacan, "Position of the Unconscious," *Écrits*, trans. Bruce Fink (New York and London: W.W. Norton & Co., 1966), 708.

39. Andrew J. Lewis, "Absolute Difference: The Trace of the Concept," *UMBR(a)*, #1(1998), 62.

40. Lacan, *The Seminar, Book XX, On Feminine Sexuality, The Limits of Love and Knowledge, Éncore*, trans. Bruce Fink (New York and London: W.W. Norton & Co., 1998), 50.

41. *The Seminar of Jacques Lacan, Book III: The Psychoses*, trans. Russell Grigg (New York and London: W.W. Norton & Co., 1993), 119.

42. Derrida, *Of Grammatology*, 324, footnote 9. If Lacan focuses on the cut, Derrida retains the pair signifier-signified in order to undo its structural closure through the work of *différance*.

43. Lacan, *The Seminar, Book III*, 32.

44. Lacan, "The Signification of the Phallus," *Écrits*, 579.

45. An unconscious symptom thus pointing not to some deep hidden truth, as Best and Marcus would have it, but to an articulation of the signifying chain. See Lacan, "On the Subject Who Is Finally in Question," *Écrits*, 194.

46. Sigmund Freud, *Three Essays on Sexuality, The Standard Edition of the Complete Psychological Works*, Vol. VII, Trans. James Strachey (London: The Holgarth Press, 1953), 168.

47. Alenka Zupančič, *Why Psychoanalysis? Three Interventions* (Denmark: NSU Press, 2008), 16. See Jean Laplanche, *Life and Death in Sexuality*, trans. Jeffrey Mehlman (Baltimore and London, The Johns Hopkins University Press, 1976), chapters 1&2.

48. Alenka Zupančič, *What Is Sex?*, (Cambridge, MA and London: The MIT Press, 2017), 30.

49. Zupančič, *Why Psychoanalysis?*, 18.

50. Cassandra B. Seltman, "Too Much of Not Enough: An Interview with Alenka Zupančič," *Los Angeles Review of Books*, March 9, 2018.

51. Jacques Lacan, "Subversion of the Subject," *Écrits*, 689.

52. Jacques Lacan, "The Signification of the Phallus," *Écrits*, 579–80.

53. Lacan, "The Signification of the Phallus," 580–81. Lacan writes that in Freud's formulations "the phallus is not a fantasy, if we are to view fantasy as an imaginary effect. Nor is it as such an object . . . inasmuch as 'object' tends to gage the reality involved in a relationship. Still less is it the organ — penis or clitoris — that it symbolizes. And it is no accident that Freud adopted as a reference the simulacrum it represented to the Ancients." 579. For the phallus is a signifier, Lacan says, a signifier that has no signified, *The Seminar, Book XX*, 81.

54. Jacqueline Rose, *Feminine Sexuality: Jacques Lacan and the école freudienne*, ed. Juliet Mitchell and Jacqueline Rose, trans. Jacqueline Rose (New York and London: W.W. Norton & Co., 1982), 40.

55. Rose, 49.

56. Rose, 42.

57. Lacan, "The Signification of the Phallus," 580.

58. Lacan, 580–81.

59. Lacan, *The Seminar, Book XX*, 74. See Joan Copjec, "Sex and the Euthanasia of Reason," *Read My Desire: Lacan against the Historicists* (Cambridge, MA and London: The MIT Press, 1994).

60. Lacan, *Television: A Challenge to the Psychoanalytic Establishment*, ed. Joan Copjec, trans. Denis Hollier, Rosalind Kraus, and Annette Michelson (New York and London: W.W. Norton, 1990), 3.

61. Lacan, *Television*, 40–41.

62. Peggy Kamuf, *A Derrida Reader: Between the Blinds*, ed. Peggy Kamuf (New York: Columbia University Press, 1991), 464.

63. Barbara Johnson, "The Frame of Reference: Poe, Lacan, Derrida," *The Purloined Poe: Lacan, Derrida, and Psychoanalytic*

Reading, eds. John P. Muller and William J. Richardson (Baltimore and London: The Johns Hopkins University Press, 1088), 217.

64. Lacan, "Seminar on 'The Purloined Letter'," *Lacan, Derrida, and Psychoanalytic Reading*, trans. Jeffrey Mehlman, eds. John P, Muller and William J. Richardson (Baltimore and London: The Johns Hopkins University Press, 1988), 28, 29.

65. Lacan, 39.

66. Jacques Derrida, "The Purveyor of Truth," *Yale French Studies* 52 (1975), 45. Citations are from this, Derrida's complete essay; the version in *The Purloined Poe* is abridged.

67. Derrida, 31.

68. Derrida 94–95.

69. Derrida, 95, 45.

70. Derrida, 63.

71. Derrida, 63.

72. Johnson, "The Frame of Reference," 218.

73. Johnson's puzzlement is put into relief by her closing comment attributing her own frame of reference "to a very large extent" to the writings of Lacan and Derrida, 250, as well as by her translation of, and brilliant introduction to *Dissemination*.

74. Lacan, "Seminar on 'The Purloined Letter'," 53.

75. Derrida, "The Purveyor of Truth," 66.

76. Johnson, "The Frame of Reference," 227.

77. The glossary of *Reading Capital* defines the problematic thusly: "A word or concept cannot be considered in isolation; it only exists in the theoretical or ideological framework in which it is used: its problematic. . . . It is not the essence of the thought of an individual or epoch which can be deduced from a body of texts by an empirical, generalizing reading; it is centered on the *absence* of problems and concepts within the problematic as much as their presence. . . ." Ben Brewster, "Glossary," in Louis Althusser, and Etienne Balibar, *Reading Capital*, translated by Ben Brewster. London and New York: Verso, 1970, 326.

78. Derrida, "Positions": Interview with Jean-Louis Houdebine and Guy Scarpetta, *Positions*, trans. Alan Bass (Chicago: The

University of Chicago Press, 1981), 80. Interview first published in *Promesse* 30–31(1971).

79. Derrida, 107–13, footnote 44.

80. Derrida, "Le Facteur de la verité," in *The Postcard: From Socrates to Freud and Beyond*, trans. Alan Bass (Chicago: The University of Chicago Press, 1987). "Le Facteur" originally appeared in *Poétique*, 21 (1975).

81. Jacqueline Rose, *Sexuality in the Field of Vision* (London and New York: Verso, 1986), 18.

82. Jacques Derrida and Elisabeth Roudinesco, *For What Tomorrow . . . A Dialogue*, trans. Jeff Fort (Stanford, Stanford University Press: 2004), 171.

83. Roudinesco, *Jacques Lacan*, 172.

84. Derrida, "Positions": Interview, 172.

85. Derrida, "Le Facteur de la verité," *The Postcard: From Socrates to Freud and Beyond*, trans. Alan Bass (Chicago: The University of Chicago Press, 1987).

86. Rose, *Sexuality in the Field of Vision*, 21.

87. Derrida, *The Postcard*, 356.

88. Derrida, "Necessity Is the Drive," *UMBR(a)* #1 (1997).

89. Jacques Derrida and Jean-Luc Nancy, "'Eating Well.' Or the Calculation of the Subject," trans. Peter Connor and Avital Ronell, *Who Comes after the Subject?* ed. Eduardo Cadava, Peter Connor, Jean-Luc Nancy (New York and London: Routledge, 1991), 103–04.

90. Marx, Capital: A Critical Analysis of Capitalist Production, Vol. 1, ed. Frederick Engels, translated by Samuel Moore and Edward Aveling. New York: International Publishers, 2003, 504.

91. I use here Johnson's translation of the French, *Écrits*, 692.

92. Derrida, "The Purveyor of Truth," 94.

93. Johnson, 244. Following Johnson's reading, Lacan, like Marx, sees a dislocation in the sentence, but unlike the bourgeois economists who unconsciously join together two incommensurable terms, Lacan exposes them.

94. *The Seminar of Jacques Lacan, Book XI: The Four*

Fundamental Concepts of Psychoanalysis, trans. Alan Sheridan (New York and London: W.W. Norton & Co., 1981), 207.

95. Johnson, "The Frame of Reference," 244.

96. Johnson, 244–45.

97. Johnson, 245.

98. Johnson, 242.

99. Lacan, *The Seminar, Book XX*, 72.

100. Jacques Derrida, *Spurs: Nietzsche's Styles*, in Peggy Kamuf, A *Derrida Reader*, 358 (selected for Kamuf's translation). For the complete text with both French and English, see *Spur's: Nietzsche's Styles/Éperons: Les Styles de Nietzsche*, trans. Barbara Harlow (Chicago and London: The University of Chicago Press, 1979).

101. Derrida, 362, 370.

102. Derrida, 374. "Style" as stylus or spur functions in the text as a complex metaphor of the tearing of the veil of "truth."

103. Geoffrey Bennington, *Interrupting Derrida* (London and New York: Routledge, 2000), 96.

104. Bennington, 96.

105. Bennington, 97.

106. Derrida, "Différance," 26.

107. Derrida, "Freud and the Scene of Writing," 212.

108. Sigmund Freud, "Beyond the Pleasure Principle," *The Standard Edition*, Vol. XVIII, 60.

109. Derrida, "To Speculate — on 'Freud'," *The Postcard*, 383–85.

110. Freud, *Three Essays on Sexuality*, 61, note 1.

111. Bennington, 106.

112. Bennington, 107, 108.

113. Bennington, 109.

114. Johnson, "The Frame of Reference," 245.

115. Roudinesco, *For What Tomorrow*, 172.

116. Paul de Man, *Allegories of Reading: Figural Language in Rousseau, Nietzsche, Rilke, and Proust*, (New Haven and London: Yale University Press, 1979), 299; cited in Rose, *Sexuality in the Field of Vision*, footnote 29, 18.

117. de Man, 298.
118. Derrida, "Différance," 22.
119. Derrida, 20–21.
120. Derrida, "The Double Session," *Dissemination*, 220.
121. Kamuf, *A Derrida Reader*, xiv.
122. Johnson, "Translator's Introduction," xxvii.
123. Derrida, *Dissemination*, 221.
124. J. Laplanche and J.-B. Pontalis, *The Language of Psycho-Analysis*, trans. Donald Nicholson-Smith (New York and London: W.W. Norton & Co., 1973), 249–50.
125. J. Laplanche, *Life and Death in Psychoanalysis*, 16. Laplanche doesn't like "anaclisis," used as a translation of the German *Anlehnung*. He uses "étayage" in *Vie et mort en psychanalyse*; Jeffrey Mehlman uses "propping" in the English translation.
126. Laplanche, 19.
127. Zupančič, *What Is Sex?*, 30.
128. *The Seminar of Jacques Lacan, Book XI*, 167.
129. Zupančič cites Lacan's words from Seminar XVIII, currently not published in English: "Discourse begins from the fact that there is a gap here. . . . But, after all, nothing prevents us from saying that it is because discourse begins that the gap is produced. It is a matter of complete indifference toward the result. What is certain is that discourse is implied in the gap." Lacan, *Le Séminaire, livre XVIII: D'un discours qui ne serait pas du semblant* (Paris: Seuil, 2006), 107; cited in *What Is Sex?*, 41.
130. Zupančič, 41–42.
131. Zupančič, 42. Although Lacan aligns the Real with the impossible, he cautions prudence, suggesting that "the best way of approaching these notions is not to take them by negation," negation suggesting the "possible" as the other of the impossible (*The Seminar, Book XI*, 167). Zupančič aims to avoid this problem with her formulation of the way the minus-one "curves" the discursive structure.
132. Zupančič, 42–43.
133. Zupančič, 48. "Surplus enjoyment" plays, of course,

with Freud's understanding of sexuality as "human deviation" from vital needs. Zupančič comments that Lacan came late to situating loss within the signifying order itself, and in doing so came closer to Freud's notion of primary repression (48–49).

134. Zupančič, 49.

135. Rose, *Feminine Sexuality*, 40. Lacan's move away from the anatomical reality picks up on Freud's own consideration of the symbolic value of the phallus and its relation to castration and the Oedipus complex. See "Phallus" in Laplanche and Pontalis.

136. Rose, 43.

137. See *Le Séminaire XXII*, January 21, 1975, in *Ornicar*.

138. Rose, *Feminine Sexuality*, 48.

139. Frida Saal, "Lacan ◊ Derrida," transcribed lecture.

140. de Man, *Allegories of Reading*, 298.

141. Derrida, "Différance," 20.

142. Derrida, "Necessity Is the Drive, *UMBR(a)*, #1 (1997): 165.

143. The "knowledge" here would be "*savoir*," symbolic knowledge of the unconscious. "*Connaissance*" pertains to the imaginary register of the ego.

The question of immanence raises the question of Gilles Deleuze's relationship to Lacan. There are reasons to argue that Deleuze's readings are closer to the Lacanian Real than some assume. See Daniel W. Smith, "The Inverse Side of the Structure: Žižec on Deleuze on Lacan," *Criticism* 46 no. 4 (2004) for a review of the debates.

144. Johnson, "The Frame of Reference," 244.

145. Zupančič, *What Is Sex*, 42.

146. Zupančič, 49. See Zupančič's discussion, pp. 44–62, which shows how Lacan's formulations correspond to Freud's thinking on the libido as masculine.

3. Reading the Stamp of History

1. Walter Benn Michaels, "Meaning and Affect, Phil Chang's *Cache Active*," https://nonsite.org/meaning-and-affect-phil-changs-cache-active/.

For the rich and entangled relationship between Tom McCarthy and Simon Critchley, see Michaels, *The Beauty of a Social Problem: Photography, Autonomy, Economy* (Chicago and London: The University of Chicago Press, 2015), 197.

2. Stephen Best and Sharon Marcus, "Surface Reading: An Introduction," *Representations* 108 (Fall 2009), 3–4.

3. Michaels's reference is to Lacan, "The Function and Field of Speech and Language in Psychoanalysis," in *Écrits*, trans. Bruce Fink (New York and London: W.W. Norton & Co., 1966), 262.

4. Michaels cites Douglas Crimp, *On the Museum's Ruins*, (Cambridge: The MIT Press, 1993), 155, 154, 167.

5. As Marx famously writes in a prosopopeia that evokes the West African "fetish" as fantasmatically imagined by mercantile traders: "Could commodities themselves speak, they would say: Our use-value may be a thing that interests men. It is no part of us as objects. What, however, does belong to us as objects is our value. Our natural intercourse as commodities proves it. In the eyes of each other we are nothing but exchange values." Karl Marx, *Capital: A Critical Analysis of Capitalist Production*, Vol. 1, ed. Frederick Engels, trans. Samuel Moore and Edward Aveling (New York: International Publishers, 2003), 87.

6. Michaels, *The Beauty of a Social Problem*, 67.

7. Michaels, *The Beauty of a Social Problem*, 41. Michaels is citing Nicholas Brown in conversation. He refers elsewhere to Brown's "The Work of Art in the Age of its Real Subsumption under Capital," March, 2012, https://nonsite.org/the-work-of-art-in-the-age-of-its-real-subsumption-under-capital/.

For Michaels's further discussion of Cheng's work and of other artists of Cheng's generation, see "Neoliberal Aesthetics" and "The Experience of Meaning" in *The Beauty of a Social Problem*.

8. In Michaels's writings, "art" refers to works of artistic production, but also to the more general category of critical distance, hence his attention to textual critique as well as to artistic and literary work.

9. See Michaels, ". . . the political meaning of the refusal

of form... is the indifference to those social structures that, not produced by how we see, cannot be overcome by seeing differently. And it's this refusal of form and embrace of vision that are at the heart of neoliberal aesthetics." *The Beauty of a Social Problem*, 63. It is for this reason that "diversity" supports neoliberalism and reinforces capitalism's reach.

10. Proponents of post-critique fail to point out that what Paul Ricoeur opposes to "suspicion" is a theological hermeneutics based on "a confidence in language: belief that language, which bears symbols, is not so much spoken by men as spoken to men, that men are born into language, into the light of the logos 'who enlightens anyone who comes into the world.'" Paul Ricoeur, *Freud & Philosophy: An Essay on Interpretation*, trans. Denis Savage (New Haven and London: Yale University Press, 1970), 29–30.

11. Althusser, Louis and Etienne Balibar. *Reading Capital*, trans. Ben Brewster (London and New York: Verso, 1970), 17.

12. Derrida, *Dissemination*, translated by and introduction by Barbara Johnson. Chicago, The University of Chicago Press, 1981. 221; and "Différance," *Margins of Philosophy*, translated by Alan Bass. Chicago: The University of Chicago Press, 1982. 22.

13. See Marx's 1859 preface to *A Contribution to the Critique of Political Economy*, ed. Maurice Dobb, translated by S.W. Ryazanskaya. Moscow: Progress Publishers, 1970.

14. "Glossary," 319. See Freud's crucial development of *Uberdeterminierung*. It is the notion of overdetermination that enables Althusser to theorize the Marxist totality as a "structure in dominance" as against the (more legible) expressive totality of base and superstructure. See *Reading Capital*.

15. Foucault's analysis of the epistemological break owes much to Marx as well as to Gaston Bachelard and Althusser. Althusser was indebted, of course, to Lacan, for whom Marx announces that "history inaugurates another dimension of history and opens up the possibility of completely subverting the function of discourse as such, and properly speaking, of philosophical

discourse, inasmuch as it rests on a conception of the world." Lacan, *The Seminar of Jacques Lacan, Book XX: On Feminine Sexuality, The Limits of Love and Knowledge, Éncore*, trans. Bruce Fink (New York and London: W.W. Norton & Co., 1998), 32–33.

16. Best and Marcus, "Surface Reading," 16.

17. A conflictual theory would involve inherent ruptures, as in the rupture of meaning and being.

18. Louis Althusser, "On Freud and Marx," *Rethinking Marxism: A Journal of Economics, Culture and Society*, 4 no. 1 (1991), 19. Quoted in Agon Hamza, "Lacan contra Althusser: Dialectical Materialism vs. Nominalism," *Continental Thought and Theory: A Journal of Intellectual Freedom* 1, no. 1, http://ctt.canterbury.ac.nz/.

19. Levi Bryant, Nick Srnicek and Graham Harman, eds., *The Speculative Turn: Continental Materialism and Realism* (Melbourne: re.press, 2011), 1 and back cover.

20. Bryant, Srnicek, and Harman, 3.

21. Quentin Meillassoux, *After Finitude: An Essay on the Necessity of Contingency*, trans. Ray Brassier (London and New York: Bloomsbury Academic, 2008), 5.

22. Jane Bennett, *Vibrant Matter: A Political Ecology of Things* (Durham, Duke University Press, 2010), ix.

23. Zupančič, *What Is Sex?* (Cambridge, MA and London: The MIT Press, 2017), 76.

24. Levi Bryant, *The Democracy of Objects* (Ann Arbor: Open Humanities Press, 2011), 13–33. See his "The Ontic Principle: Outline of an Object-Oriented Ontology" in *The Speculative Turn*, 261–78. Influenced by Deleuze, Bryant postulates being as difference: "To be is a simple binary, insofar as something either is or is not. If something makes a difference then it is, full stop," something that epistemology forgets," 268. He agrees, paraphrasing Heidegger, that epistemology "always and everywhere proceeds on this basis as a pre-epistemological comprehension of difference," 264.

25. Meillassoux, *After Finitude*, 4.
26. Meillassoux, 28.
27. Meillassoux, 10.
28. Meillassoux, 125.
29. Meillassoux., 33.
30. Meillassoux, 125.
31. Meillassoux, 34, 125.
32. Zupančič, *What Is Sex?*, 76.
33. Zupančič, 47.
34. Zupančič, 76, 78, quoting Lacan, *Le Séminaire, livre XVI, D'un autre à l'Autre* (Paris: Seuil, 2006), 33.
35. See *Le Séminaire de Jacques Lacan, livre XVIII. D'un discours qui ne serait pas du semblant* (Paris: Seuil, 2006), 28.
36. Zupančič, *What Is Sex?*, 80.
37. Zupančič, 81, citing Lacan, *Le Sémainaire, livre XVIII*, 28.
38. Zupančič, 76.

The Lacanian Real is not the only counter to the new materialists. For those who wish to escape correlationism, there is, indeed, no escaping tiresome language, for with the break of modern science, verbal language emerges ever more fully as a formalist operation akin to mathematics. That is, its habitually referential function is increasingly revealed as an unstable effect of formalist signification rather than of psychologism or logocism. This is, of course, the message of Derridean undecidability. For Derrida, undecidability is not about a something that can be decided in a referential mode, nor about an ineffable something that language strains toward, but about the (impossible) disarticulation of meaning from being. For a Derridean counter-reading of the materialist turn, see Astrid Schrader's "Haunted Measurements: Demonic Work and Time Experimentation," in which Schrader looks to the Derridean trace as a way of reading the problem of entanglement in quantum physics. In *differences* 23, no. 2 (2012).

39. Sigmund Freud, "Splitting of the Ego in the Process of Defence," *The Standard Edition*, XXIII, trans. James Stracey (London: The Holgarth Press, 1995), 276.

40. See Chapter VII of *An Outline of Psycho-Analysis, The Standard Edition*, XXIII.

41. Jacques Derrida, *Glas*, trans. John P. Leavey, Jr. and Richard Rand (Lincoln and London: University of Nebraska Press, 1986), 210.

42. J. Laplanche and J.-B. Pontalis, *The Language of Psycho-Analysis*, trans. Donald Nicholson-Smith (New York and London: W.W. Norton & Co., 1973), 119.

43. For an insightful reading of Freudian and Derridean theories of the trace see Rosaura Martînez Ruiz, "Freud and Derrida: Writing and Speculation (or When the Future Erupts in the Present)." *Filozofski vestnik*, 2015.

44. In Freud's theoretical construction of the psychic apparatus, the protective shield protects the organism from potentially harmful excitations from the outside world. As Richard writes, the mnemic trace can be sensory, but also the trace of a thought, especially a verbal thought.

45. François Richard, "Mnemic Trace/Memory Trace," *International Dictionary of Psychoanalysis*, encyclopedia.com.

46. Freud, *Three Essays on the Theory of Sexuality, The Standard Edition, Vol. VII*, trans. James Strachey (London: The Holgarth Press, 1995) 154, footnote 2.

47. The original French title *Spectres de Marx* was expanded in the 1994 English edition to *Specters of Marx: The State of the Debt, the Work of Mourning, & the New International*, trans. Peggy Kamuf (New York and London: Routledge, 1994).

48. See Tom Lewis, "The Politics of 'Hauntology' in Derrida's *Specters of Marx*," Jacques Derrida, Terry Eagleton, Fredric Jameson, Antonio Negri et al., *Ghostly Demarcations: A Symposium on Jacques Derrida's Specters of Marx.* (London and New York: Verso, 1999).

49. Derrida, *Specters of Marx*, 151.

50. Marx, Capital: A Critical Analysis of Capitalist Production, Vol. 1, ed. Frederick Engels, translated by Samuel Moore and Edward Aveling. New York: International Publishers, 2003. 76.

51. Here I use a different translation of *Capital* in order to accommodate some of Derrida's readings, which hew close to the German. Marx, *Capital: A Critique of Political Economy, Vol. I*, trans. Ben Fowkes (London: Penguin Classics, 1990), 163.

52. Marx, *Capital*, trans. Moore and Aveling, 77.

53. Derrida, *Specters of Marx*, 160.

54. Derrida, *Specters of Marx*, 150.

55. Fredric Jameson, "Marx's Purloined Letter," Jacques Derrida, Terry Eagleton, Fredric Jameson, Antonio Negri et al., *Ghostly Demarcations: A Symposium on Jacques Derrida's Specters of Marx* (London and New York: Verso, 1999), 36.

56. Jameson, 37.

57. Jameson, 36.

58. Lacan, *Le Séminaire, livre XVI*, 1–25. Lacan stresses here and elsewhere that the relationship is homologous, not analogous.

59. The four discourses are each represented as algorithms, each containing four algebraic symbols standing for the master signifier, knowledge, the subject, and surplus enjoyment. For readings that see the shift from the master's discourse to the university discourse as having to do with social shifts under capitalism, see Justin Clemens and Russell Grigg, eds., *Jacques Lacan and the Other Side of Psychoanalysis: Reflections on Seminar XVII* (Durham and London: Duke University Press, 2006).

60. Lacan, *Le Séminaire, livre XVI*, 20.

61. Lacan, *The Seminar of Jacques Lacan, Book XVII: The Other Side of Psychoanalysis*, trans. Russell Grigg (New York and London: W.W. Norton & Co., 2007), 78.

62. Lacan, *Le Séminaire*, livre XVI, 20–21.

63. Lacan, *Le Séminaire*, livre XVI, 21.

64. Alenka Zupančič, "When Surplus Enjoyment Meets Surplus Value," *Reflections on Seminar XVII*, 159.

65. Lacan, *The Seminar, Book XVII*, 51.

66. Lacan, *The Seminar, Book XVII*, 45, 44.

67. Luce Irigaray, *This Sex Which Is Not One*, trans. Catherine Porter (Ithaca: Cornell University Press, 1985).

4. Reading the Feminist Impossible

1. Timothy Bewes, "Reading with the Grain: A New World in Literary Criticism," *differences* 21, no. 3 (2010): 1.

2. It was the meeting of critique and identity politics that Naomi Schor evoked in her naming of the journal *differences*, a name that captures the collision of French theoretical *difference* and U.S. multicultural *differences*.

3. Among numerous examples, see Denise Riley, *"Am I That Name?" Feminism and the Category of "Women" in History* (Minneapolis: University of Minnesota Press, 1988); Wendy Brown, "The Impossibility of Women's Studies," *differences* 9, no. 3 (1997); and Andrea Long Chu, "The Impossibility of Feminism," *differences* 30, no. 1 (2019).

4. Zupančič, "When Surplus Enjoyment Meets Surplus Value," *Reflections on Seminar XVII: Jacques Lacan and the Other Side of Psychoanalysis*, eds. Justin Clemens and Russell Grigg (Durham and London: Duke University Press, 2006), 171.

5. Samo Tomšič, *The Capitalist Unconscious: Marx and Lacan* (London and New York: Verso, 2015), 38–39.

6. Marx, *Capital: A Critique of Political Economy, Vol. I*, trans. Ben Fowkes (London: Penguin Classics, 1990), 255.

7. Tomšič, *The Capitalist Unconscious*, 219–20. At a conference in Milan in 1972, Lacan speaks of the capitalist discourse as a "fifth discourse."

8. Michaels, "Meaning and Affect: Phil Chang's *Cache Active*." Nonsite.org, https://nonsite.org/meaning-and-affect-phil-changs-cache-active/.

9. Zupančič, "When Surplus Enjoyment Meets Surplus Value," 173, 177.

Coda

1. Sedgwick, "Paranoid Reading and Reparative Reading," in *Novel Gazing: Queer Readings in Fiction* (Durham: Duke University Press, 1997), 131, 144.

2. Samia Vasa, "2002: A Reading Appeal," special issue "–30– The End of the Story," *differences* 30, no. 3 (2019).

3. Andrea Long Chu, *Females* (London and New York: Verso, 2019).

4. Stephen Best, *None Like Us: Blackness, Belonging, Aesthetic Life* (Durham and London: Duke University Press, 2018). Best cites Lee Edelman, "Against Survival: Queerness in a Time That's Out of Joint," *Shakespeare Quarterly* 62, no. 2 (2011): 162.

5. Thangham Ravindranathan, *Behold an Animal: Four Exorbitant Readings* (Evanston: Northwestern University Press, 2020).

6. Vasa footnotes the question with the following: "Lacan says about this mood of *knowing*: 'When the space of a lapsus no longer carries any meaning (or interpretation), then only is one sure that one is in the unconscious. *One knows*.'" Lacan, *The Seminar, Book XI*, vii.

7. Walter Benn Michaels, *Our America: Nativism, Modernism, and Pluralism* (Durham and London: Duke University Press, 1995), 141. Michel de Certeau, "Vocal Utopias: Glossolalias," *Representations* 56 (Autumn 1996): 31.

8. David Walker, *Appeal to the Coloured Citizens of the World*, ed. Peter P. Hinks (University Park: Pennsylvania State University Press, 2012).

9. Valerie Solanas, *SCUM Manifesto* (London: Verso, 2004).

10. Coined by sexologist Ray Blanchard to mean "love of oneself as a woman." Blanchard, "The Classification and Labeling of Nonhomosexual Gender Disphorias," *Archives of Sexual Behavior*, 18, no. 4 (1989): 315–34. It is for this reason, Chu writes, that sissy porn is popular with many in that the fetish objects involved ("make-up, lingerie, breasts, high heels, and the color pink") *promise* castration rather than warding against it. And as for feminism, the desire for it is also desire, structured by fantasy, meaning "something you believe in not because it is true but because you want to. . . . Feminism's being impossible doesn't keep us feminists from wanting it. . . . If you like, we can call it

the Impossibility of Not-Feminism." Chu, "The Impossiblity of Feminism," *differences* 30, no. 3 (2019): 78.

11. Eric Chrevillard, *Sans l'orang-outan* (Paris: Minuit, 2007). Chapter 2 of Ravindranathan, *Behold an Animal* is "Man of the Forest: Eric Chrevillard, with La Fontaine and Poe."

12. Jean Baudrillard, *Impossible Exchange*, trans. Chris Turner (London: Verso, 2001), 16.

13. Ravindranathan describes the work of the animal "as more thoroughly described in the exorbitance with which it affects the entirety of a text's meanings." The reader might find this exorbitance reflected in Baudrillard's words on cosmic emergence cited in the epilogue: "This emergence out of the void, this *non-anteriority of things to themselves* continue[s] to affect the event of the world at the very heart of its historical unfolding," (emphasis Ravindranathan). Of course, the non-anteriority of things to themselves carries strong associations with the Derridean "impossible inaugurality/originary supplementarity," Ravindranathan notes, going on to remark "that it is extremely difficult, in fact, to distinguish or extricate the question of the animal, in Derrida's writing, from the movement of deconstruction itself."

Bibliography

Abel, Elizabeth, Barbara Christian, and Helene Moglen, editors. *Female Subjects in Black and White: Race, Psychoanalysis, Feminism*. Berkley, Los Angeles, and London: University of California Press, 1997.

Adams, Parveen, and Elizabeth Cowie. *The Woman in Question: m/f*. Cambridge, MA: The MIT Press, 1990.

Althusser, Louis. "On Freud and Marx." *Rethinking Marxism: A Journal of Economics, Cutlure and Society* 4, no. 1 (1991).

Althusser, Louis and Etienne Balibar. *Reading Capital*, translated by Ben Brewster. London and New York: Verso, 1970.

Baudrillard, Jean. *Impossible Exchange*, trans. Chris Turner. London: Verso, 2001.

Bell, Derrick. *And We Are Not Saved: The Elusive Quest for Racial Justice*. New York: Basic Books, 1987.

Bennett, Jane. *Vibrant Matter: A Political Ecology of Things*. Durham, Duke University Press, 2010.

Bennington, Geoffrey. *Interrupting Derrida*. London and New York: Routledge, 2000.

Berger, Anne. "Sexing Differances," special issue "Derrida's Gift," *differences* 16, no. 3 (2005).

Best, Stephen and Sharon Marcus, "Surface Reading: An Introduction," *Representations* 108 (Fall 2009).

Best, Stephen. *None Like Us: Blackness, Belonging, Aesthetic Life*. Durham and London: Duke University Press, 2018.

Bewes, Timothy. "Reading with the Grain: A New World in Literary Criticism," *differences* 21, no. 3 (2010).

Blanchard, Ray. "The Classification and Labeling of Nonhomosexual Gender Disphorias." *Archives of Sexual Behavior*, 18, no. 4 (1989).

Brook, Eloise. "Trans, transgender, cisgender: we are what we name ourselves," The Conversation, August 11, 2014. http://theconversation.com.

Brown, Wendy. *States of Injury: Power and Freedom in Late Modernity*. Princeton: Princeton University Press, 1995.

——. "The Impossibility of Women's Studies," *differences* 9, no. 3 (1997).

Bryant, Levi. *The Democracy of Objects*. Ann Arbor: Open Humanities Press, 2011.

Bryant, Levi, Nick Srnicek and Graham Harman, eds., *The Speculative Turn: Continental Materialism and Realism*. Melbourne: re.press, 2011.

Butler, Judith. *Gender Trouble: Feminism and the Subversion of Identity*. New York and London, Routledge, 1990.

Chevillard, Eric. *Sans l'orang-outan*. Paris: Minuit, 2007.

Chu, Andrea Long. *Females*. London and New York: Verso, 2019.

——. "The Impossibility of Feminism," *differences* 30, no. 1 (2019).

Clemens, Justin and Russell Grigg, eds. *Jacques Lacan and the Other Side of Psychoanalysis: Reflections on Seminar XVII*. Durham: Duke University Press, 2006.

Copjec, Joan. "Sex and the Euthanasia of Reason," *Read My Desire: Lacan against the Historicists*. Cambridge, MA and London: The MIT Press, 1994.

Crimp, Douglas. *On the Museum's Ruins*. Cambridge: The MIT Press, 1993.

de Certeau, Michel. "Vocal Utopias: Glossolalias,"
Representations 56 (Autumn 1996).
de Man, Paul. *Allegories of Reading: Figural Language in Rousseau, Nietzsche, Rilke, and Proust*. New Haven and London: Yale University Press, 1979.
———. *Blindness and Insight*. Minneapolis, University of Minnesota Press, 1983.
Derrida, Jacques. "Différance," *Margins of Philosophy*, translated by Alan Bass. Chicago: The University of Chicago Press, 1982.
———. *Dissemination*, translated by and introduction by Barbara Johnson. Chicago, The University of Chicago Press, 1981.
———. "Freud and the Scene of Writing," *Writing and Difference*, translated by Alan Bass. Chicago: The University of Chicago Press, 1978.
———. *Glas*, translated by John P. Leavey, Jr. and Richard Rand (Lincoln and London: University of Nebraska Press, 1986.
———. *Learning to Live Finally: The Last Interview*, translated by Michael Nass and Pascale-Anne Brault. Brooklyn and London: Melville House, 2007.
———. "Le Facteur de la vérité," *The Postcard: From Socrates to Freud and Beyond*, translated by Alan Bass. Chicago: The University of Chicago Press, 1987.
———. "Letter to a Japanese Friend," *Psyche: Inventions of the Other, Vol. II*, edited by Peggy Kamuf and Elizabeth Rottenberg. Stanford: Stanford University Press, 2008.
———. "Necessity Is the Drive," *UMBR(a)* #1 (1997).
———. *Of Grammatology*, translated by Gayatri Chakravorty Spivak (Baltimore and London: The Johns Hopkins University Press, 1976.
———. "Positions": Interview with Jean-Louis Houdebine and Guy Scarpetta, *Positions*, translated by Alan Bass (Chicago: The University of Chicago Press, 1981.
———. "Signature, Event, Context," *Limited Inc.*, translated by Samuel Weber and Jeffrey Mehlman. Evanston, IL: 1988.

———. *Specters of Marx: The State of the Debt, the Work of Mourning, & the New International*, translated by Peggy Kamuf. New York and London: Routledge, 1994.

———. *Speech and Phenomena and Other Essays on Husserl's Theory of Signs* (Evanston, IL: Northwestern University Press, 1973.

———. *Spurs: Nietzsche's Styles*, edited by Peggy Kamuf. In *A Derrida Reader: Between the Blinds*. New York: Columbia University Press, 1991.

———. "The Purveyor of Truth," *Yale French Studies* 52, 1975.

Derrida, Jacques and Christie V. McDonald, Interview, "Choreograhies," special issue "Cherchez la Femme: Feminist Critique/Feminist Text," *diacritics* 12, no. 2 (1982).

Derrida, Jacques and Elisabeth Roudinesco, *For What Tomorrow . . . A Dialogue*, translated by Jeff Fort. Stanford, Stanford University Press: 2004.

Derrida, Jacques and Jean-Luc Nancy, "'Eating Well.' Or the Calculation of the Subject," translated by Peter Connor and Avital Ronell, *Who Comes after the Subject?* ed. Eduardo Cadava, Peter Connor, Jean-Luc Nancy. New York and London: Routledge, 1991.

Derrida, Jacques, Terry Eagleton, Fredric Jameson, Antonio Negri, et al. *Ghostly Demarcations: A Symposium on Jacques Derrida's Specters of Marx*. London and New York: Verso, 1999.

Dosse, François. *History of Structuralism, Vol. 1*, translated by Deborah Glassman. Minneapolis and London: University of Minnesota Press, 1997.

———. *History of Structuralism, Vol. 2: The Sign Sets, 1967–Present*, translated by Deborah Glassman. Minneapolis and London: University of Minnesota Press, 1997.

Douglass, Patrice D. "Black Feminist Theory for the Dead and Dying," *Theory and Event* 21, no. 1 (2018).

du Cille, Ann. "'The Occult of True Black Womanhood: Critical Demeanor and Black Feminist Studies," *Female Subjects in Black and White: Race Psychoanalysis Feminism*, ed. Elizabeth Abel, Barbara Christian, and Helene Moglen. Berkeley: University of California Press, 1997.

Edelman, Lee. "Against Survival: Queerness in a Time That's Out of Joint," *Shakespeare Quarterly* 62, no. 2 (2011).

———. *Bad Education: Why Queer Theory Teaches Us Nothing*. Durham and London: Duke University Press. 2022.

Eltis, David. "Europeans and the Rise and Fall of African Slavery in the Americas: An Interpretation," *American Historical Review* 98, no. 5 (1993).

Felman, Shoshana, ed. Special issue "Literature and Psychoanalysis. The Question of Reading: Otherwise," *Yale French Studies* 55/56 (1977).

Foucault, Michel. *The Birth of Biopolitics: Lectures at the Collège de France 1978–79*, ed. Michel Senellart, translated by Graham Burchell. New York: Palgrave Macmillan, 2008.

———. *The Order of Things: An Archaeology of the Human Sciences*, translated by Alan Sheridan. New York: Vintage Books, 1970.

Freud, Sigmund. *An Outline of Psychoanalysis. The Standard Edition, Vol. XXIII*, translated by James Stracey. London: The Holgarth Press, 1995.

———. *Beyond the Pleasure Principle. The Standard Edition, Vol. XVIII*, translated by James Strachey. London: The Holgarth Press, 1995.

———. "Splitting of the Ego in the Process of Defence," *The Standard Edition, Vol. XXIII*, translated by James Stracey. London: The Holgath Press, 1995.

———. *Three Essays on the Theory of Sexuality*, *The Standard Edition, Vol. VII*, translated by James Strachey. London: The Holgarth Press, 1995.

Hamza, Agon. "Lacan contra Althusser: Dialectical Materialism vs Nominalism," *Continental Thought and Theory: A Journal of Intellectual Freedom* 1, no. 1. http://ctt.canterbury.ac.nz/.

Hartman, Saidiya. "The Position of the Unthought": An Interview with Saidiya Hartman Conducted by Frank B. Wilderson III., *Qui Parle*, 13, no. 2 (2003).

Hull, Akasha Gloria, Patricia Bell-Scott and Barbara Smith, eds. *All the Women Are White All the Blacks Are Men but Some of Us Are Brave: Black Women's Studies*. Old Westbury N.Y: Feminist Press, 1982.

Irigaray, Luce. *An Ethics of Sexual Difference*, translated by Carolyne Burke and Gillian C. Gill. Ithaca, NY: Cornell University Press, 1993.

———. *This Sex Which Is Not One*, translated by Catherine Porter. Ithaca: Cornell University Press, 1985.

Jameson, Fredric. "Marx's Purloined Letter," Jacques Derrida, Terry Eagleton, Fredric Jameson, Antonio Negri et al, *Ghostly Demarcations: A Symposium on Jacques Derrida's Specters of Marx*. London and New York: Verso, 1999.

Johnson, Barbara. "The Frame of Reference: Poe, Lacan, Derrida," *The Purloined Poe: Lacan, Derrida, and Psychoanalytic Reading*, ed. John P. Muller and William J. Richardson. Baltimore and London: The Johns Hopkins University Press, 1988.

———. "Translator's Introduction," in Derrida, Jacques, *Dissemination* trans. Barbara Johnson. Chicago, The University of Chicago Press, 1981.

———. "Women and Allegory," *The Wake of Deconstruction*. Cambridge, MA: Blackwell Publishers, 1994.

———. "Writing," *Critical Terms for Literary Study*, ed. Frank Lentricchia and Thomas McLaughlin. Chicago and London: The University of Chicago Press, 1995.

Johnston, Adrian. "The Symbolic," Lacan.com.

Joyrich, Lynne. "TV Trumps," *Unwatchable*, ed. Nicholas Baer, Maggie Hennefeld, Laura Horek, and Gunnar Iverssen. New Brunswick, NJ: Rutgers University Press, 2019.

Kamuf, Peggy. *A Derrida Reader: Between the Blinds*, ed. Peggy Kamuf. New York: Columbia University Press, 1991.

Krašovek, Primož. "Neoliberal Epistemology—From the Impossibility of Knowing to Human Capital," *Philozofija I Društvo* 24, no 4 (2013).

Lacan, Jacques. *Le Séminaire de Jacques Lacan, livre XVI. D'un autre à l'Autre.* Paris: Seuil, 2006.

———. *Le Séminaire de Jacques Lacan, livre XVIII. D'un discours qui ne serait pas du semblant.* Paris: Seuil, 2006.

———. "Position of the Unconscious," *Écrits*, translated by Bruce Fink, New York and London: W.W. Norton & Co., 1966.

———. "Seminar on 'The Purloined Letter'," translated by Jeffrey Mehlman, *Lacan, Derrida, and Psychoanalytic Reading*, eds. John P, Muller and William J. Richardson. Baltimore and London: The Johns Hopkins University Press, 1988.

———. *Television: A Challenge to the Psychoanalytic Establishment*, ed. Joan Copjec, translated by Denis Hollier, Rosalind Kraus, and Annette Michelson. New York and London: W.W. Norton, 1990.

———. "The Function and Field of Speech and Language in Psychoanalysis." In *Écrits*, trans. Bruce Fink. New York and London: W.W. Norton & Co., 1966.

———. "The Instance of the Letter in the Unconscious," *Écrits*, translated by Bruce Fink. New York and London: W.W. Norton & Co., 1966.

———. *The Seminar of Jacques Lacan, Book III: The Psychoses*, translated by Russell Grigg. New York and London: W.W. Norton & Co., 1993.

———. *The Seminar of Jacques Lacan, Book VII: The Other Side of Psychoanalysis*, translated by Russell Grigg. New York and London: W.W. Norton & Co. 2007.

———. *The Seminar of Jacques Lacan, Book XI: The Four Fundamental Concepts of Psychoanalysis*, translated by Alan Sheridan. New York and London: W.W. Norton & Co., 1981.

———. *The Seminar of Jacques Lacan, Book XX: On Feminine Sexuality, The Limits of Love and Knowledge, Éncore*, translated by Bruce Fink. New York and London: W.W. Norton & Co., 1998.

———. "The Signification of the Phallus," *Écrits*, translated by

Bruce Fink. New York and London: W.W. Norton & Co., 1966.

Laplanche, Jean. *Life and Death in Psychoanalysis*. translated by Jeffrey Mehlman. Baltimore and London: The Johns Hopkins University Press, 1976.

Laplanche, J. and J.-B. Pontalis, *The Language of Psycho-Analysis*, translated by Donald Nicholson-Smith. New York and London: W.W. Norton & Co., 1973.

Latour, Bruno. "Why Has Critique Run out of Steam? From Matters of Fact to Matters of Concern," *Critical Inquiry* 30 (Winter 2004): 226–28.

Lewis, Andrew J. "Absolute Difference: The Trace of the Concept," *UMBR(a)*, #1 (1998).

Lewis, Tom. "The Politics of Hauntology in Derrida's *Spectres of Marx*," Jacques Derrida, Terry Eagleton, Fredric Jameson, Antonio Negri et al, *Ghostly Demarcations: A Symposium on Jacques Derrida's Specters of Marx*. London and New York: Verso, 1999.

Marcus, Sharon, Heather Love, and Stephen Best, "Building a Better Description," *Representations* 135 (Summer 2016).

Marriott, David S. *Lacan Noir: Lacan and Afro-pessimism*. Switzerland: Palgrave Macmillan, 2021.

Marx, Karl. *Capital: A Critical Analysis of Capitalist Production*, Vol. 1, ed. Frederick Engels, translated by Samuel Moore and Edward Aveling. New York: International Publishers, 2003.

———. *Capital: A Critique of Political Economy, Vol. I*, translated by Ben Fowkes. London: Penguin Classics, 1990.

Meillassoux, Quentin. *After Finitude: An Essay on the Necessity of Contingency*, translated by Ray Brassier. London and New York: Bloomsbury Academic, 2008.

Michaels, Walter Benn. *The Beauty of a Social Problem: Photography Autonomy Economy*. Chicago Illinois: University of Chicago Press, 2015.

———. "Meaning and Affect: Phil Chang's *Cache Active*." Nonsite.org, https://nonsite.org/meaning-and-affect-phil-changs-cache-active/.

———. *Our America: Nativism, Modernism, and Pluralism* (Durham and London: Duke University Press, 1995)

Michaels, Walter Benn and Adolph Reed Jr. *No Politics but Class Politics*, edited by Anton Jäger and Daniel Zamora. New York: Columbia University Press, 2023.

Nichols, Robert. *The World of Freedom: Heidegger, Foucault, and the Politics of Historical Ontology*. Stanford: Stanford University Press, 2014.

Patterson, Orlando. *Slavery and Social Death: A Comparative Study*. Cambridge: Harvard University Press, 1982.

Peeters, Benoît. *Derrida: A Biography*, translated by Andrew Brown. Cambridge U.K. and Malden, MA: Polity Press, 2013.

Ravindranathan, Thangam. *Behold an Animal: Four Exorbitant Readings*. Evanston: Northwestern University Press, 2020.

Readings, Bill. *The University in Ruins*. Cambridge: Harvard University Press, 1996.

Richard, François. "Mnemic Trace/Memory Trace," *International Dictionary of Psychoanalysis*, encyclopedia.com.

Ricoeur, Paul. *Freud & Philosophy: An Essay on Interpretation*, translated by Denis Savage. New Haven and London: Yale University Press, 1970.

Riley, Denise. *"Am I That Name?" Feminism and the Category of "Women" in History*. Minneapolis: University of Minnesota Press, 1988.

Roden, David. "The Subject," *Understanding Derrida: An Invitation to Philosophy*, ed. Jack Reynolds and Jonathan Roffe. London and New York: Continuum, 2004.

Rose, Jacqueline. *Feminine Sexuality: Jacques Lacan and the école freudienne*, ed. Juliet Mitchell and Jacqueline Rose, translated by Jacqueline Rose. New York and London: W.W. Norton & Co., 1982.

———. "Donald Trump's victory is a disaster for modern masculinity," *The Guardian*, Nov. 15, 2016.

———. *Sexuality in the Field of Vision*. London and New York: Verso, 1986.

Roudinesco, Elisabeth. *Jacques Lacan*, translated by Barbara Bray. New York: Columbia University Press, 1997.

Ruiz, Rosaura Martînez. "Freud and Derrida: Writing and Speculation (or When the Future Erupts in the Present." *Filozofski vestnik*, 2015

Saal, Frida. "Lacan ◊ Derrida," transcription from a speech at the Tenth Symposium of the Fundacion Mexicana de Psicoanálisis, on *Writing and Psychoanalysis*, February 1994.

Schrader, Astrid. "Haunted Measurements: Demonic Work and Time Experimentation," *differences* 23, no. 2 (2012).

Scott, Joan W. *Gender and the Politics of History*, Revised Edition. New York: Columbia University Press, 1999.

———. "Gender: A Useful Category of Historical Analysis," *Gender and the Politics of History*. New York: Columbia University Press, 1988.

———. *Only Paradoxes to Offer: French Feminisms and the Rights of Man*. Cambridge, MA and London: Harvard University Press, 1996.

Sedgwick, Eve Kosofsky, "Paranoid Reading and Reparative Reading." In *Novel Gazing: Queer Readings in Fiction*. Durham: Duke University Press, 1997.

———. *Touching Feeling: Affect, Pedagogy, Performativity*. Durham: Duke University Press, 2006.

Seltman, Cassandra B. "Too Much of Not Enough: An Interview with Alenka Zupančič." *Los Angeles Review of Books*, March 9, 2018.

Seshadri-Crooks, Kalpana. *Desiring Whiteness: A Lacanian Analysis of Race*. New York and London: Routledge, 2000.

Sexton, Jared. "Afro-Pessimism: The Unclear Word," *Rhizomes: Cultural Studies in Emerging Knowledge* 29 (2016).

———. *Amalgamation Schemes*. Minneapolis: Minneapolis University Press, 2008.

Smith, Daniel W. "The Inverse Side of the Structure: Žižec on Deleuze on Lacan," *Criticism* 46 no. 4 (2004).

Solanas, Valerie. *SCUM Manifesto*. London: Verso, 2004.

Spillers, Hortense J. "Afro Pessimism and Its Others," The New

School Institute for Critical Social Inquiry lecture, June 9, 2021.

———. "'All the Things You Could Be by Now if Sigmund Freud's Wife Was Your Mother': Psychoanalysis and Race," *Black and White and in Color*. Chicago and London: The University of Chicago Press, 2003.

———. "Mama's Baby, Papa's Maybe: An American Grammar Book," *Black, White, and in Color*. Chicago and London: The University of Chicago Press, 2003.

———. "'Whatcha Gonna Do'? Revisiting 'Mama's Baby, Papa's Maybe: An American Grammar Book'": A Conversation with Hortense Spillers, Saidiya Hartman, Farah Jasmine Griffin, Shelley Eversley, & Jennifer L. Morgan, *Women's Studies Quarterly* 35, nos. 1&2 (2007).

Tomšič, Samo. *The Capitalist Unconscious: Marx and Lacan*. London and New York: Verso, 2015.

Vasa, Samia. "2002: A Reading Appeal," special issue "–30– The End of the Story," *differences* 30, no. 3 (2019).

Walker, David. *Appeal to the Coloured Citizens of the World*, edited by Peter P. Hinks. University Park: Pennsylvania State University Press, 2012.

Weed, Elizabeth and Naomi Schor, eds. *Feminism Meets Queer Theory*. Bloomington and Indianapolis: Indiana University Press, 1997.

Weheliye, Alexander G. "Black Studies and Black Life," *The Black Scholar* 44, no. 2 (2014).

Wilderson III, Frank B. *Red, White & Black: Cinema and the Structure of U.S. Antagonisms*. Durham & London: Duke University Press, 2010.

———. "Without Priors," *The Big No*, ed. Keenan Ferguson. Minneapolis and London: University of Minnesota Press, 2021. Sexton

Zupančič, Alenka. *Ethics of the Real: Kant and Lacan*. London and New York: Verso, 2000.

———. *What Is Sex?* Cambridge, MA and London: The MIT Press, 2017.

———. "When Surplus Enjoyment Meets Surplus Value," *Reflections on Seminar XVII: Jacques Lacan and the Other Side of Psychoanalysis*, ed. Justin Clemens and Russell Grigg. Durham and London: Duke University Press, 2006.

———. *Why Psychoanalysis? Three Interventions*. Denmark: NSU Press, 2008.

Index

academic feminism: decline of, 2–3, 5; difference vs. differences divide in, 32–33; post-critique, 3–5, 9, 40; post-1960s branches of, 42–43; post-structuralist- and psychoanalytic-influenced, 2, 5–7, 44–46; and surface reading, 39
Adams, Parveen, 142n1
Afro-pessimism, 10–13, 17–19, 136n25, 140n62
alienation, 15–16, 60–61, 73
All the Women Are White, All the Men Are Black, But Some of Us Are Brave (anthology), 18
Althusser, Louis, 23, 67–68, 98, 99, 115, 148n77, 154n14, 154n15
animals, 129–30
art, as criticism, 92–94, 96–97, 123–24

Barthes, Roland, 2, 8
Baudrillard, Jean, 130, 161n13
being: blacks and, 11–12, 14, 16–17; Derrida and, 81; as difference, 155n24; meaning disjoined from, 6, 96, 99, 106, 119, 156n38; modern conceptions of, 6; women in relation to, 52–53. *See also* ontology
Bell, Derrick, 34
Benet, Alfred, 110–11
Bennett, Jane, 100
Bennington, Geoffrey, 77–79
Berger, Anne, 54
Best, Stephen, 7–9, 28, 37, 39, 90, 94–95, 97–98, 126–28
Bewes, Timothy, 120
binary oppositions, 3, 46, 48, 52–53, 88, 155n24
black feminism, 17–19, 43, 138n43
#BlackLivesMatter, 7, 10, 34, 138n43
blacks/blackness: and bodies, 13–14; critique grounded in experience of, 10–21; and gender, 13–14, 17–21; ontological status of, 11–12, 14, 16–17; violence experienced by, 10–12

175

Black Scholar, The (journal), 9
black studies, 10, 127–28
Bonaparte, Marie, 65–66
Brook, Eloise, 35
Brown, Nick, 93
Brown, Wendy, 25–26, 159n3
Bryant, Levi, 99–101, 155n24
Butler, Judith, 14, 19, 46, 121

capitalism: art as critical of, 92–94, 96–97, 123–24; effects of, 9; feminism and, 123; historical stamp of, 90, 93–94, 97; and impossibility, 121–22; logic of, 25, 39; Marx's surface reading of, 96–97; neoliberalism and, 9, 90, 93; surface reading in relation to, 9, 94. *See also* alienation; commodification
castration, 38, 60, 62, 64, 66, 76, 85–88, 107, 123–24, 128, 152n135
catachresis, 19–21
certainty. *See* knowledge; sexual certainty; truth
Chang, Phil, 90–93, 96–97
Chevillard, Eric, 129–30
Chu, Andrea Long, 126, 128–29, 159n3, 160n10
closure: disruption of, 7, 8, 51; feminist responses to problem of, 43–44; metaphysical, 54, 74; phallic, 5, 6, 47
COINTELPRO, 135n17
Combahee River Collective, The (anthology), 143n4
commodification, 21–23, 92–93, 98
commodity fetishism, 22, 38–39, 111–14, 122, 153n5
Copernicus, Nicolaus, 102
Copjec, Joan, 147n59
correlationism, 100–101, 103, 156n38
Coward, Rosalind, 142n1
Cowie, Elizabeth, 142n1

Crimp, Douglas, 91
Critchley, Simon, 90
critique: black studies and, 10–13; contemporary forms of, 126–30; critiques of, 4–5, 8–9, 37, 39–40, 100; "gender" as category of, 3, 19–20, 46, 121; identity in tension with, 120–21; need for, 125; neoliberalism's challenge for, 25; and the production of meaning, 8–9; reading the impossible as practice of, 29, 89, 121–24, 126–30. *See also* post-critique

de Certeau, Michel, 128
decolonization, 10
deconstruction: and binary oppositions, 3; feminism and, 45–46, 90; as form of surface reading, 94–96; Lacanian theory contrasted with, 62; metaphysics and, 63, 79; psychoanalysis and, 46, 79–80; as reading strategy, 51, 87. *See also* poststructuralism
Deleuze, Gilles, 152n143, 155n24
de Man, Paul, 34, 37, 79, 80, 86–87
demystification. *See* critique
depth. *See* surface vs. depth frame
Derrida, Jacques: and the animal, 161n13; and being, 81, 106; critique of metaphysics by, 46, 50–51, 54, 63, 72, 77–80; *différance* concept of, 9, 46, 51–52, 54, 66, 70, 78, 81–82, 86, 96, 109, 116; "Le Facteur de la verité," 49, 62–63, 68, 70, 72, 76; and the feminine, 52–53, 62, 76–77; and fetishism, 106–9; and Freud, 62–63, 68–70, 77–81, 86, 106–9; and identity, 70; Lacan compared to, 47–50, 55–88, 144n17; and Marx, 111–15;

reading strategy of, 50, 54–55, 67, 72–73, 80, 86–87, 96, 98; and sexual difference, 29, 40, 46–62, 106; and the stamp of history, 106, 119; the subject as theorized by, 55–56, 68–70, 72, 80, 116, 118–19; and undecidability, 52–53, 63, 76–83, 89, 96, 106–8, 110, 112, 119, 156n38
Descartes, René, and Cartesianism, 100, 101, 103
description, as critical strategy, 28, 39, 123–24
desire, 16, 59–60, 86, 107, 128–29
différance, 9, 46, 51–52, 54, 66, 70, 78, 81–82, 86, 96, 109, 116
difference/differences divide, 32–33, 47–48, 89
differences (journal), 159n2
discourse, 116–19, 124, 151n129, 158n59
dissemination, 52–53, 66, 73
diversity, 35, 121, 140n62, 154n9
Dosse, François, 49
Douglass, Patrice, 17–19
Drucker, Peter, 27, 140n63
Du Cille, Ann, 21–22

Edelman, Lee, 138n46, 160n4education. *See* academic feminism; higher education
Eltis, David, 135n18
empathy, 26
epistemology: feminism and, 5; modern, 5–6, 25, 27–28, 90. *See also* knowledge
essentialism, 3, 21–22, 44
exchange value, 153n5

Fanon, Frantz, 10, 17
Felman, Shoshana, 46
Female Subjects in Black and White (anthology), 21

feminine. *See* woman and the feminine
feminism: Afro-pessimism and, 17; and capitalism, 123; and epistemology, 5; and gender critique, 19–20; impossibility associated with, 90, 121, 123–24, 160n10; in the neoliberal era, 120–24; queer theory and, 120–21; and sexual difference, 31–32; socialist, 43, 142n1, 143n4; transgender and, 3, 32–33. *See also* academic feminism; black feminism
fetishism: commodity, 22, 38–39, 111–14, 122, 153n5; Freud and, 106–11; sexual, 38–39; in thinking/knowing, 37–40
Foucault, Michel, 1, 5, 23–24, 27, 154n15
Freud, Sigmund: annexation and revision of theories of, 99; Derrida and, 62–63, 68–70, 77–81, 86, 106–9; and fetishism, 106–11; Lacan and, 6, 47–49, 56–58, 63–65, 106–7, 152n133, 152n146; and metaphysics, 63, 69, 77–80, 83; model of the psychic apparatus, 109–10, 145n36, 157n44; and the phallus, 147n53, 152n135; reading strategy of, 95–96; and screen memories, 110–11; and sexuality, 47, 58–59, 84; and the subject, 47, 56; and the unconscious, 57–59, 63, 81, 83, 119

Gaines, Korryn, 18–19, 137n38
gap: covering of, 8, 61, 85, 123; critical opportunity provided by, 121, 124, 126; epistemological, 8; meaning/signification characterized by, 9, 29, 84–85, 87, 118, 121, 124, 126; in the subject, 61, 118

gender: black critique of, 13–14, 17–21; as a category, 3, 120, 121; as category of critique, 3, 19–20, 46, 121; conservative/authoritarian attacks on, 3, 36; as an identity, 3, 5, 35–39, 121; multiplicity of, 32–33, 36–39; political uses of, 3, 20, 30–31; sexual difference in relation to, 20; sexuality/biology in relation to, 3, 31, 33, 46, 120–21. *See also* identity/identities
gender studies, 3, 13, 36
ghosts and spectrality, 111–13
Goldmann, Lucien, 1–2
Gujarat riots, 126–27

Harman, Graham, 99–100
Hartman, Saidiya, 10, 26, 136n25
Hayek, Frederick, 24, 27–28, 140n63
Hegel, G.W.F., 53, 101, 107, 114–15
Heidegger, Martin, 70, 72, 155n24
Hume, David, 102
Husserl, Edmund, 55
hymen, 52–53, 76, 82

identity/identities: certainty about, 33, 35; "constitutive" politics of, 34, 35–36; "contractual" politics of, 34; critique in tension with, 120–21; deconstruction and, 46, 50–52; Derrida and, 70; gender as, 3, 5, 35–39, 121; multiplicity of, 32–33, 36–39; natural grounds of, 25, 33; neoliberalism and, 25–26; the other as essential for, 26; politics of, 25–26, 33–35; subjective grounds of, 33, 35. *See also* post-identity
impossibility: capitalism and, 121–22; critical engagement with, 29, 89, 121–24, 126–30; desire and attempts to expunge, 121–24; of the feminist project, 90, 121, 123–24, 160n10; of knowledge, 39, 106; the Lacanian Real and, 84, 105–6, 119, 151n131; of meaning, 16; reading of, 29, 89; of sexual difference, 5–7, 17, 29, 32, 40, 77, 86, 121; structural interpretations of, 118
in-itself, 101–2
injury, 25–26
interpretation. *See* reading
Irigaray, Luce, 15, 31, 119

Jakobson, Roman, 2
James, C.L.R., 10
Jameson, Fredric, 95, 114–15
Johnson, Barbara, 8, 34–37, 46, 50, 52, 63, 66–67, 72–75, 77, 79, 82, 87, 124, 148n73
Johnston, Adrian, 145n37
jouissance, 16, 61–62, 117–18, 124
Joyrich, Lynne, 134n7

Kamuf, Peggy, 63, 82
Kant, Immanuel, 5, 101–3
Klein, Melanie, 65
knowledge: fetishistic, 37–40; Freud's concept of the unconscious and, 80, 83; impossibility of, 39, 106. *See also* epistemology; truth
Krašovec, Primož, 27–28

Lacan, Jacques: on altruism and victimization, 26; and being, 106; black studies and, 10, 14–16; and capitalism, 123; Derrida compared to, 47–50, 55–88, 144n17; and desire, 59–60; and the feminine, 16,

62, 65, 76–77; and fetishism, 106–7; and Freud, 6, 47–49, 56–58, 63–65, 106–7, 152n133, 152n146; and the imaginary and the symbolic, 136n30; and knowing, 160n6; and lack, 14–17, 60, 64–65, 84–85, 107, 117; and Marx, 115–19, 154n15; and *objet a*, 86, 116, 118–19; reading strategy of, 50, 80, 86, 96; and the Real, 16–17, 29, 77, 83–89, 100, 104–6, 119, 151n131, 156n38; Rome Discourse, 15; on rupture of meaning and being, 6, 16; "Seminar on 'The Purloined Letter,'" 62–67, 98; and sexual difference, 29, 40, 47–62, 84–86, 106; and the stamp of history, 106, 119; and structuralism, 1–3, 9; the subject as theorized by, 15, 47, 55–56, 58, 61, 63, 68–69, 72, 74, 85–87, 117–19; and the symbolic order, 9, 15–16, 47, 56, 58, 60–61, 63, 65, 85, 91, 145n37; and truth, 62, 65

lack: Derrida and, 65–66; Lacanian concept of, 14–17, 60, 64–65, 84–85, 107, 117

language: Derrida and, 51, 81, 116; Lacan and, 85, 116; rupture of meaning and being in, 6; structural interpretations of, 5; and the subject, 15, 55–56; transparency of, 35; and the unconscious, 56. *See also* meaning

Laplanche, Jean, 83, 108

Latour, Bruno, 4

LAXART, 90

Lewis, Andrew, 56

liberalism, 23–24, 43, 44. *See also* neoliberalism

linguistic turn, 100

logocentrism, 51, 68, 78. *See also* phallogocentrism

Love, Heather, 39

Mallarmé, Stéphane, 52, 82, 96

Marcus, Sharon, 7–9, 28, 37, 39, 90, 94–95, 97–99

Marriott, David, 10, 15–17, 29

Marx, Karl: on commodity fetishism, 21–23, 28, 38–39, 111–14, 122–23, 153n5; contribution of, to political economy, 12, 22, 68, 72–73, 97; Derrida and, 111–15; Lacan and, 115–19, 154n15; and the stamp of history, 22–23, 97, 139n53; surface reading practiced by, 96–97

Marxism: basic principles of, 97, 99, 115; black critique and, 10; and commodification, 25; death of, 112; deconstruction and, 114–15; feminism and, 43, 45, 120; psychoanalysis and, 116; theory of history, 1

materialism, 114–15. *See also* new materialisms

materiality, 90–92

May '68 events, 1, 115–16

McCarthy, Tom, 90

McDonald, Christie, 54

meaning: being disjoined from, 6, 96, 99, 106, 119, 156n38; Derrida's conception of, 51–52, 81, 86; Derrida's critique of, 77–80; impossibility of, 16; Lacan's conception of, 65; modern conceptions of, 6; in neoliberal era, 91–92; paranoid blocking of, 8, 125; production of, 8–9; structures of, 5; surface reading and, 98; the unconscious and, 6–7, 57. *See also* language; truth

Meillassoux, Quentin, 100–105
metaphysics: Derrida's critique of, 46, 50–51, 54, 63, 72; Freud and, 63, 69, 77–80, 83; skepticism about, 102; speculation and, 103; and truth, 6
metapsychology, 69–70, 79–80, 83
m/f (journal), 43–46, 142n1
Michaels, Walter Benn, 90–94, 96–98, 119, 123–24, 127, 153n9
misogyny, 6–7, 17, 29–31, 128
misreading, 98–99
modernity, and epistemology, 5–6, 25, 27–28, 90
Moynihan Report, 13

Nancy, Jean-Luc, 72
naturalization, 4, 25–26
negation, 151n131
neoliberalism: Afro-pessimism and, 140n62; capitalism and, 9, 90, 93; and critique or post-critique, 9, 28, 90, 121; Derrida's criticism of, 111; discursive ground of, 25, 27–28; feminism and, 120–24; and identity politics, 25; meaning in era of, 91–92; truth as transactional in, 25, 36; as way of being and thinking, 23–24
new materialisms, 99, 105–6, 156n38. *See also* materialism
new realism. *See* new materialisms; political realism
Nichols, Robert, 11–12
Nietzsche, Friedrich, 25, 76

objet a, 86, 116, 118–19
ontology: Afro-pessimist critique of, 11–12; Derridean critique of, 50–51; object-oriented discourses and, 100–101. *See also* being
Orbán, Viktor, 3, 36

otherness: identity and, 26; masculine/feminine binary and, 43, 46, 88; subjectivity and, 47, 49, 56, 61; the unconscious and, 57
overdetermination, 45, 90, 154n14

paranoid reading, 8, 125
Patterson, Orlando, 10, 12, 135n18
phallogocentrism, 47, 51–52, 65–66, 71, 73, 76, 88, 116
phallus, 39, 59–62, 64–66, 70, 72–74, 85–86, 107, 123–24, 147n53, 152n135
philosophy. *See* science vs. philosophy
Plato, 52, 82
Poe, Edgar Allan, 130; "The Purloined Letter," 62–67, 98
Polanyi, Michael, 27, 140n63
political realism, 8, 94
Pontalis, J.-B., 83, 108
postal principle, 70
post-critique, 9, 24, 89–90, 94–106, 134n14, 154n10
post-identity, 140n60
postmodernism, 91–93
post-structuralism, 3, 5. *See also* deconstruction
problematic, 67–68, 148n77
prohibition, 47, 60
psychoanalysis: deconstruction and, 46, 79–80; Derrida and, 70–72, 78–79; feminism and, 2, 5–7, 44–45, 90; as form of surface reading, 94–96; Lacan's critique of, 15; Marxism and, 116; the subject as theorized by, 44–45, 47, 80–81. *See also* Freud, Sigmund; Lacan, Jacques
Putin, Vladimir, 3

queer theory, 20, 120–21, 138n43

Ravindranathan, Thangam, 126, 129–30, 161n13
reading: Afro-pessimism as, 12–13; critical, 29; Derrida's strategy of, 50–51, 54–55, 67, 72–73, 80, 86–87, 96, 98; Freud's strategy of, 95–96; of impossibility, 29, 89; Lacan's strategy of, 50, 80, 86, 96; in the neoliberal era, 9; paranoid, 8, 125; sexual difference and, 54; the stamp of history, 90; strategies of, 7–8; symptomatic, 67–68, 98; theories vs. modes of, 95. *See also* misreading; surface reading
Real, the, 16–17, 29, 77, 83–89, 100, 104–6, 119, 151n131, 156n38
realism: political, 8, 94; speculative, 99–101
Redding, Bill, 24
Reed, Adolph, 25
representation, 5, 90–91
ressentiment, 25–26
Richard, François, 109–10
Ricoeur, Paul, and suspicion, 154n10
Riley, Denise, 159n3
Roden, David, 55
Rose, Jacqueline, 14, 30–31, 60, 68, 70, 80, 85–86, 126
Roudinesco, Elisabeth, 1–2, 48, 68–69, 79, 83, 109, 119
Rousseau, Jean-Jacques, 80
Russian formalism, 2

Saal, Frida, 55, 86
Saussure, Ferdinand de, 56–57
#SayHerName, 7, 138n43
Schor, Naomi, 159n2
Schrader, Astrid, on Derridean trace and quantum physics, 156n38
science vs. philosophy, 102–4

Scott, Joan, 19–20, 46, 121
screen memories, 110
Sedgwick, Eve, 4, 8, 125
Seshadri-Crooks, Kalpana, 14
Sexton, Jared, 10, 11–13, 138n43
sexual certainty, 30–33, 39–40. *See also* truth
sexual difference: contemporary debates over, 32; Derrida and, 29, 40, 46–62, 106; feminism and, 31–32; gender in relation to, 20; impossibility of, 5–7, 17, 29, 32, 40, 77, 86, 121; Lacan and, 29, 40, 47–62, 84–86, 106; opposition to, 31; problematization of, 43–44; reading and, 54. *See also* sexual certainty
sexual fetishism, 38–39
the signifier, 2, 9, 56–58, 63–64, 70, 73–75, 84–85, 87–88, 117–18
signifying order, 29, 84–85, 88, 117–18, 121, 124, 126, 152n133
socialist feminism, 43, 142n1, 143n4
Solanas, Valerie, 128–29
Sollers, Phillipe, 48
Sontag, Susan, 90
spectrality. *See* ghosts and spectrality
speculative realism, 99–101
Spillers, Hortense, 10, 13–14, 136n25, 137n35
Spivak, Gayatri, 45–46
Srnicek, Nick, 99–100
stamp of history: capitalism and, 90, 93–94, 97; Chang's *Cache, Active* and, 91–93, 96–97; commodification as outcome of, 22, 139n53; critique and, 90; defined, 22; Derrida and, 106, 119; as interpretive framework, 25; Lacan and, 106, 119; Marx and, 22–23, 97, 139n53; reading of, 90–93, 106

Stirner, Max (professional name of Johann Casper Schmidt), 112
structuralism, 1–3, 5–6, 115–16
structural linguistics, 5
structures and structural relations: black critique and, 10–13, 15; as conditions of the possibility of meaning production, 9; French theory and, 1–2, 5–6, 9; humanist opposition to, 1–2; Lacan and, 1–2, 6, 9; May '68 events and, 1–2; of meaning, 5; ontological, 11–12; substitution of the relational for, 26
subjectivity/the subject: Derridean conception of, 55–56, 68–70, 72, 80, 116, 118–19; Freudian conception of, 47, 56; Lacanian conception of, 15, 47, 55–56, 58, 61, 63, 68–69, 72, 74, 85–87, 117–19; language and, 15, 55–56; object-oriented discourses and, 101; otherness and, 47, 49, 56, 61; psychoanalytic conceptions of, 44–45, 47, 80–81; the signifier and, 74; theories of unified, 44, 47; the unconscious and, 47, 56
sufficient reason, 102
surface reading: annexation and revision of, 99; characteristics of, 7–8, 37, 94, 99; critical passivity imputed to, 9, 28, 94, 98; critique of critique from standpoint of, 8, 28, 37; deconstruction and, 94–96; and freedom, 9, 98; Marx and, 96–97; and meaning, 98; as misreading, 98; new materialisms and, 106; psychoanalysis and, 94–96; and stamp of history, 90
surface vs. depth frame, 94–98
surplus *jouissance*, 116–19, 151n133, 158n64

surplus value, 116, 118–19
survival, 54–55, 71, 81, 116
symbolic order, Lacan's concept of, 9, 15–16, 47, 56, 58, 60–61, 63, 65, 85, 91, 145n37
symptomatic reading, 67–68, 98

Tel Quel (journal), 48
TERFs, 3
This Bridge Called My Back (anthology), 143n4
Tompkins, Silvan, 8
Tomšič, Samo, 122–23
trace, the, 48, 51, 54, 55, 63, 81, 96, 109, 116
transgender: concept of gender challenged by, 20; critique associated with, 128–29; feminism and, 3, 32–33; opposition to, 36
Trump, Donald, 30–31
truth: jouissance and, 117; Lacan and, 62, 65; language as transparent to, 35; modernity's challenge to, 6, 8; as natural/objective, 33; post-truth era and, 4; sexual identities and, 32–39; as subjective, 33–39; transactional character of, 25, 36; women in relation to, 52–53. *See also* knowledge; meaning; sexual certainty

the unconscious: Derrida and, 81; Freud and, 57–59, 63, 81, 83, 119; language and, 56; meaning and, 6–7, 57, 160n6; otherness and, 57; sexuality and, 58; and subjectivity, 47, 56
undecidability, 52–53, 63, 76–83, 89, 96, 106–8, 110, 112, 119, 156n38
United Nations (UN) Conference on Women (1995), 20

universality, critique of, 18
use value, 39, 112–14, 153n5
US House of Representatives, 20

Vasa, Samia, 126–27
victimization, 25–26
violence: blacks subjected to, 10–12; black women subjected to, 138n43; sexual, 126–27; women subjected to, 18

Walker, David, 128
Weheliye, Alexander, 10
Wilderson, Frank, 10–17, 19, 136n25, 140n62
woman and the feminine: being and truth in relation to, 52–53; as a category, 121; Derrida and, 52–53, 62, 76–77; jouissance belonging to, 61–62; Lacan and, 16, 62, 65, 76–77; Nietzsche and, 76; violence against, 18
womanist theory, 121
Women's March on Washington, 18
Wynter, Sylvia, 18, 21

Yale School, 45–46

Žižek, Slovoj, 79
Zupančič, Alenka, 26, 29, 58–59, 83–85, 88, 100, 104–6, 117, 118, 121–22, 124, 126, 151n131, 152n133, 152n146

Elizabeth Weed is Director Emerita of the Pembroke Center for Teaching and Research on Women at Brown University and editor of *differences: A Journal of Feminist Cultural Studies*.

www.ingramcontent.com/pod-product-compliance
Lightning Source LLC
Chambersburg PA
CBHW020412080526
44584CB00014B/1289